# PRECISION PURPOSE

## Enjoying the

## *Signature Life*

## You

## Were Born to Live!

# PRECISION PURPOSE

## Enjoying the

## *Signature Life*

## You

## Were Born to Live!

## Osazee O. Thompson

Precision Purpose: Enjoying the Signature Life You Were Born to Live

# *DEDICATION*

This book is dedicated all those who desire to live their dream.

To all those who may have tried and failed at something but have never quit.

To all those who desire to live their best life.

To all those who have yet to release their full potential.

This book is for you, written so that you will release the full potential inside of you, accomplish every goal, live every dream and actualize every vision that God has so graciously given you!

-Make Purpose Your Priority!

# ACKNOWLEDGEMENTS

I would like to acknowledge and recognize the following people who have had a tremendous impact on my life and have made a profound and indelible impression in my life that will never be forgotten and who also can in part take credit for the person that I am today.

First to the many family members, close friends, Pastors, teachers, professors and instructors who have been so crucial and critical in my development throughout the years. I am equally grateful to my Evbuoma family both here in the United States and in Nigeria who have embraced me and shown me tremendous love and support.

I would like to acknowledge and thank you Dr. Bill Winston for your diligence in teaching believers how to live independent of this world system, to be fearless and how to attain our inheritance and destiny by faith and to see ourselves as God sees us in the earth. For this I am eternally appreciative.

To my mother E. Jean Thompson for your continued and unending love and support throughout my life and for raising me selflessly, to be fearless, determined, to never settle for average but to always press for the best in life. I will forever be grateful to you for your Godly rearing in my life.

To my beloved wife, Antoinette, thank you for your support and encouragement. You are the epitome of the term help-meet, you have enhanced my life and been an instrumental part of me fulfilling my purpose and reaching the destination that God has called me to and for that I am forever grateful.

To my beautiful daughter, Malaika, you have a tremendous purpose to fulfill and a great destiny to reach. I am inspired by your obedience and respect for authority. Our relationship further illustrates to me the relationship I have with Father God. I desire for you to continue to practice the principle of authority, always seek first God's will for your life, love God, love people, live purpose and be an impact in your world!

Lastly, but certainly not least and most important, I would like to thank you Jesus! Thank you Lord for your relentless love for me, your incomparable patience, your joy and comfort and your peace that surpasses human understanding. I credit you for placing in me the contents of this book, by your Holy Spirit you guide and teach me daily and instruct me how to live out my unique purpose and reach the expected end you have prepared for me. Thank you for the gifts, talents and abilities you have placed in me. It is my prayer and diligent effort to double and even triple the investment that you have deposited within me. I Love You Jesus and thank you for your Love!

# CONTENTS

# PREFACE

Purpose is the point of our life! All of the other events and stages of our lives culminate to execute a specific highlight to why we were born. For example, the purpose for going to culinary arts school is ultimately to become a chef. The purpose of joining the military is ultimately to serve and defend the nation. The same is true in life, there is a specific goal to be accomplished by you and until that goal is achieved then purpose has not been fulfilled in your life. An indication of our purpose can many times be associated with our strengths and unique abilities, that is to say those things that we often feel as though we have picked up naturally and seem to perform well effortlessly.

Our purpose is captured in our giftings. Once we tap into our core giftings then we can begin to see a vision emerging that will ultimately direct us into our purpose. The passion that you have will serve as fuel as you travel on your journey to reaching your destiny. As you read this book, take time to write down the unveiled clues that will assist you on your journey to discovering your unique purpose so that you will one day reach the tremendous destiny that you were born to accomplish.

Let us begin by first giving a few modern definitions of the word purpose.


**𝔓urpose** could be defined as...

- *An intended or desired result.*

- *An original intent by a designer:*

- *The point for which a goal has been established.*

- *The motive for which any action is executed.*

- *The fulfillment of a word spoken or a deed done.*

- *The explanation by reason of why in relation to the existence of all matter seen and unseen.*

# Introduction

Discovering who you are, why you were born, your worth and your true potential are all captured in your purpose.

Your purpose is always captured in your giftings! God has designed it where everyone and everything in nature has the natural desire and instinct to fully release their God given ability and inner potential. Each one of us has been uniquely crafted and specifically designed to produce from the inside-out. This is evident even in nature and illustrated with the concept of the seed. Within every seed lies the potential to produce the full maturity of its kind.

Once we recognize our giftings, the only way for them to be seen by others in our lives, is to work them out! This word *work* is derived from a Greek word, *Ergon* closely related in meaning to the word energy. Energy is the capacity of any given person or object to perform work. Work can be explained as the movement by force to a specified distance or planned destination. So the amount of effort it takes for you to reach your destiny is called work and as a result of this work, your giftings and talents are developed and you become an answer to someone's problem.

As you develop and evolve into all that God has created you to be, then beware of the temptation to compare yourself, your work and your destiny to that of another. You were given a signature mark that can only be expressed by you. Do not attempt to measure your work by the work of another because we all have variant degrees and depths of capacity. Capacity is merely the ability to take, contain or hold. Capacity can be used also in exchange with the word potential ---this word potential is the latent qualities or abilities to produce something. Your unique purpose or what I like to call, your signature mark, is found in the DNA fibers of you gifts and talents.

As you read this book you will discover that there are three primary ways or indicators that will lead you to discovering your unique purpose and signature mark.

You may begin by asking yourself.... Is my work fulfilling to me?

What are my core giftings--- the things I seem to do effortlessly?

What kinds of problems keep showing up in my life?


What do others consistently seek me out for?


What kind of activities do I seem to be drawn too?


What things or activities do I enjoy volunteering for?

# CHAPTER 1

∞

## Discovering the Essence of Purpose

*According as he hath chosen us in him*
*before the foundation of the world,*
*that we should be holy and without*
*blame before him in love: -Ephesians 1:4 KJV*

This book is designed to ignite your passion and serve as fuel for you in the pursuit of your unique purpose in life and to live your signature life. Writing this book allows me the opportunity to help you, the reader in the discovery and development of your unparalleled unique purpose for living. Many people these days are walking about aimlessly, going in circles, uncertain and perplexed about what's next for them in life. There are a great percentage of people in the world who possess a genuine desire, deep down within them, to walk out their God given purpose. The problem is that for the great majority of them, there is a disconnect and an extreme inability in understanding exactly what purpose is and by extension what their unique purpose is and how to walk it out. In this book we will explore what purpose is, its operational function in our lives, how to identify your purpose and how to live your signature life.

One definition of purpose could be described as an intended or desired result. Upon my research in writing this book I have discovered that the actual word purpose was inserted in the English language around the late 13$^{th}$ century, roughly around 1250 – 1300 A.D. Its original meaning was borrowed from the Anglo-Norman word *purposer,* meaning *to intend.* The prefix, *pur-* means forth, taken from the Latin prefix, *pro-* and the second half of the word *-pose,* was linked to the Latin word *poser*, simply meaning *to put.* By amalgamating the two meanings, we would create the word purpose, meaning *'to put forth'* or *'an idea put forth'* as a fore-thought. So this means that before you were born, God had a fore-thought of you and all that you are and will become.

He had a plan for your life before you came into the world and as you discover your purpose, His fore-thought and plan for you, understand that your destiny is incomparable!

It is critical that we continue to define this word to capture greater meaning so that as we use the word later in the book it will add greater depth and understanding to the precise use of the word in its narrowed context. Upon further examination of the word purpose, and in an effort to attain a more comprehensive perceptive knowledge of its use, context and functionality, there are three other words of ancient origin that emerged.

The first word is the most contemporary of the group ---it is *Prothesis*, derived from post-classical Latin linguistics with its roots based on the ancient Greek *prosthesis* which means *'placing before'*.

As stated earlier the prefix *pur-* or *pro-* means before and the word *thesis* means a proposition stated for consideration to be discussed, proven or defended. So this could be interpreted *'a pre-planned or pre-determined theme'*. Let's continue as we discover what purpose means and by extension its place and function in our lives as we discover our signature mark.

The second word is *mah saba*, it conveyed the meaning of *thought, plan, scheme, plot, design or imagination.* This word is of ancient Hebrew origin and communicates the idea of *'a processed thought'* or *'a devised calculated plan'.*

The last of the three words historically used to describe purpose is *hepes*, an ancient Hebrew word as well, and perhaps the oldest known usage of the word that we now refer to as the word purpose in our modern-day vernacular ---it was often used in context to describe *desire, delight or pleasure.* In this instance the handling of this word that is synonymous with purpose was used to describe *'a desired, delightful or pleasurable result'* based on the will of a king, a common individual or a group.

Knowing the etymology of a word makes all the difference when using or applying it in context. Now that we've done some research to accurately define what purpose means, let's tie it all up into an expressed conceptual idea. Based on the root meanings of purpose, it is an original intent by design of a

creator, manufacturer or designer. Purpose is the point for
which any goal has been established. We could even say that
purpose is the thematic point of life, in many ways like a subject
in a sentence and its function as being the object of that
sentence. So in life, our purpose serves as the object or focal
point of our existence. Purpose then, is the very reason why we
were born. We were all a fore-thought in the mind of God and
He has prepared and equipped us all to do what He has called us
to do.

All of the other events and stages of our lives culminate to
execute a specific highlight to the reason why we were born.
The purpose of our lives could be synonymous with the theme
of our lives. If this theme is ignored, abandoned or rejected the
entire direction of a person's life is then misappropriated and all
their efforts misemployed. It has been said, that if purpose is not
know abuse is inevitable. The net effect of a life abused, is
failure, ruin and waste.

There is an ancient parable told of three men who were given an
investment of variant amounts. Each man received an
investment based on his unique ability to perform and produce a

profit. Each investment made was in the form of talents of money, a talent was simply a denomination of currency used at that time. Historians estimate that one talent was worth about two years' salary, equivalent to approximately more than one thousand dollars according to the economy of that time. To one of the men an investment of five talents was made, the second man received an investment input of two talents and the third man was entrusted with one talent. Let's just imagine those talents represented their purpose in the form of a gifting or unique ability or strength. There must then be a purpose for the gifting, unique abilities and strength being given to each of the men in this illustration.

Just as each one of the men in this illustration received a sum of talents, there are talents that have been deposited in each one of us as well, for a specific reason and unique purpose. Some are gifted in singing or acting, another is gifted in the ability to quickly and efficiently solve problems, and others are excellent at networking or creating or researching. The thing that all of these areas have in common is that in every case they all serve a specific purpose. The purpose is always captured in the giftings. Giftings represent seeds of greatness. It is only when you

*"The purpose is always captured in the gifting."*

discover the gift, embrace and develop the gift, that it will begin to work for you and produce wildly in your life. Now with this in mind let's continue the story of the three men in which investments were submitted.

The first man, which received five talents immediately went and invested his talents and gained five more talents, the second man with the two talents invested his and profited two additional talents. The third man took his one talent, buried it and produced no profit. This man was then labeled as wicked and lazy. How many times have procrastination and laziness caused you to either lose steam in your forward progress or stop moving at all on an assignment or project? This is common, however, the person who experiences victory and presses ahead to see success never quits and maintains an unrelenting attitude. In your quest to discover your purpose, do not lose sight of your primary goal, that is, to achieve success in what you were born to do. For example, the purpose for going to high school is ultimately gaining a diploma.

The purpose of attending college is ultimately to earn a degree and although there are many objectives to conquer, the single most valuable thing is attaining the degree you worked so diligently to obtain. The same is true in life, there is a specific goal to be accomplished by you and until that goal is achieved then purpose has not been fulfilled and success is not awarded. The foremost rumination in your mind should always be to carry out the theme of your life no matter the assignment or task. Remember, the seasons in your life will consistently change, the people in your life may come and go, the causes you stand for may cease but the purpose or theme of your life will always remain constant through them all.

# CHAPTER 2

∞

## Fulfilling the Passion of Your Purpose

*I press toward the mark for the prize*
*of the high calling of God in Christ Jesus.*
*-Philippians 3:14 KJV*

This chapter is exciting and written to move you to action. If you are passionate about identifying your signature mark and living on purpose, you will be thrilled to discover that this chapter is all about possessing your purpose and seizing every opportunity to live on purpose with the identity God has made you to represent. Possessing your purpose has to do with taking charge, responsibility and ownership of the life you have been given. Now is your opportunity to live your best life!

In a blaming society, where people often are reluctant to take responsibility for their own actions and decisions and are quick to place blame on someone else or something else, many people have become comfortable with failure or loss as long as there is someone or something to point the finger of blame toward.

There are very few who will stand to take ownership of a short-coming and then correct it. As you pursue purpose and take possession of your existence, you will make mistakes but remain focused and continue to move ahead.

It is important for you to take notes from your mistakes and grow thereby. There are two things that you can do with mistakes and failures that you experience in life, one, you may either reflect back on them, analyze the situation and take note of how it could have been done differently to produce a more favorable outcome or, two, you may reflect back on the events and beat yourself up about it. I suggest the first option, to analyze the situation and discover a better way to approach the given circumstance. A wise person will soon come to discover that they do not know it all and will seek the advice and counsel of one wiser, hence, a wise person will hear good counsel and increase in learning and a person with good understanding will always seek out sound counsel on matters. As you possess your purpose remain humble and know that there will be many corrections for you along the way in pursuit of your purpose.

I am told that when flying an airplane there are constant wind corrections and adjustments made to the aircraft during flight. These corrections and adjustments are all for the benefit of staying on course and ensuring that the plane and all its passengers arrive to the correct destination. As you begin to walk-out your purpose understand that it is not only you on a journey but there are also others with you and the part that you are playing is so important, that without you playing your part those others who are watching you and looking to you as an example, may suffer because you were the missing element and key component in the equation for them in some way accomplishing any given task. God has placed treasures in you that will add value to the lives of those around you.

*"God has placed treasures in you that will add value to the lives of those around you."*

When fathoming the idea of taking ownership and possessing your purpose, think of it in light of this illustration, that life being represented as a large jig saw puzzle and that each one of us has a piece to contribute to this puzzle of life. If one member does not contribute then the puzzle is not complete. You are a contributing member! Each person serving in their unique purpose is a contributing member, their contribution to the puzzle adds to its fullness and by this I simply mean, that you are a significant player in the game of life and you should always view yourself as adding value to your world. To do this takes courage as well as a change of heart and mind. Change of heart, in that you must believe that you are a gifted, talented person with great value to offer. And change of mind with regard to you re-programming your mind to think of yourself as an answer and a solution-maker. You must value the gifts and talents that you have been given and take full ownership of them by utilizing them, working diligently to master them on your journey to destiny.

It's time for you to take possession of your piece of the puzzle and contribute to your world and by extension the world at-large. Humanity is awaiting your contribution to make it all work and to participate in whatever part you have been born to participate. It is incumbent upon you to do this, no one can take your place and no one can stand proxy for you. You have been afforded the awesome responsibility to make a difference in your world. You are unique and someone needs what you have got to give. So take charge! Taking charge of your life will cause you to be courageous and bold. You must have a strong positive resolve, be single-minded and not become preoccupied with anything other than the purpose of your life.

> *"Taking charge of your life will cause you to be courageous and bold."*

As you possess your purpose and release your signature mark and presence, understand that with it comes also a strong sense of ownership. This ownership will at times draw ridicule and slander to you, however, as you endure the persecution continue to stand fast, press ahead and know that you are accomplishing your purpose.

There are a few things I would like to specifically highlight in this with relationship to you possessing your purpose. One, there must be total commitment to execute and completely fulfill what it is that you are to do. Commitment requires three essential elements that I have coined the 3 D's. The first of the three D's is discipline, mastery over oneself and the ability to remain invariable under pressure. The second D in the series of the three D's is determination, to be loyal and faithful no matter what challenges or obstacles may arise. The last D is dedication, to devote yourself to the cause; this means that you have taken away your own right to elect to abandon the cause of your purpose.

Additionally, I would like to highlight that with purpose comes vision and with vision a direction for your life begins to emerge. So your task is to take the vision from your imagination and make it tangible that it may touch the lives of others.

There are four key factors that are of tremendous merit as you release your signature mark and presence by possessing your purpose. I have listed here four steps to possessing your purpose. As you read them begin to put these four factors into practice.

There are four key steps to possessing your purpose, they are:

**Meditation** is to think on at length. To muse and mutter repetitiously. Consistently thinking on but more importantly believing in your ability to accomplish your unique purpose as you begin engaging in positive self-talk concerning who you are and how successful you are in your purpose. Understand that you are always led in the direction of your most dominant thought. Ask yourself, what am I thinking on the most? Look at your life and the answers will become evident. The state that your life currently reflects is a sum total of the decisions you have made which are a result of the thoughts you have meditated on in abundance. When you change the way you think, you change the way you perceive life. This new perception of life has an impact on your behavior and your renewed behavior will lead to new habits being formed in your life that will produce favorable outcomes for you.

The way you produce new outcomes in your life first begins with the way you think and believe, the way you think and believe impacts your perceptions, which is the way you view life. Your perceptions impact the way in which you respond to the situations you encounter in life. Your responses, or let's say your behavior, over time begins to form habits, it is the perpetual habits that you have adopted into your life that lead to the outcomes that you and I experience day-to-day. Hence, if you change your thinking, you will change your life!

All dramatic life-changes first occur with a renewed way of thinking and seeing life. When you change the way in which you see a person, place or thing, you will notice that those people, places and things begin to take on new meaning because you have adjusted the way in which you see them. This adjustment process is called renewing your mind. One of the most effective ways to do this is by meditation.

Meditation allows you to mentally see yourself fulfilling and accomplishing whatever given task you desire to accomplish or correcting any poor habits you desire to change for good. This is what God instructed Joshua to do in order to fulfill a part of his destiny as he operated in his unique purpose, in the book of Deuteronomy 1:6-9 KJV, it reads,

*Be strong and of a good courage: for unto this people shalt thou divide for an inheritance the land, which I sware unto their fathers to give them.*

*Only be thou strong and very courageous, that thou mayest observe to do according to all the law, which Moses my servant commanded thee: turn not from it to the right hand or to the left, that thou mayest prosper withersoever thou goest.*

*This book of the law shall not depart out of thy mouth; but thou shalt **meditate** therein day and night, that thou mayest observe to do according to all that is written therein: for then thou shalt make thy way prosperous, and then thou shalt have good success.*

*Have not I commanded thee? Be strong and of a good courage; be not afraid, neither be thou dismayed: for theLORD thy God is with thee whithersoever thou goest.*

In this account of scripture, Joshua is tasked with the enormous responsibility of leading the children of Israel from the desert wilderness into their prosperous and lavished promised land.

Moses, who initially led them out of Egyptian captivity, has now died, and Joshua is commissioned by God with this epic monumental task. The only way Joshua is going to accomplish this task is by seeing himself as equipped and well able to do it. God gives Joshua the key to being successful in completing this colossal feat, that key is meditation. Meditation on the written word of God! As Joshua was obedient to follow exactly what God had prescribed, he was successful in leading the children of Israel out of the wilderness and into their promised land. Just as Joshua was successful in his purpose so can you be successful in fulfilling your unique purpose and reaching your destiny. You must first ask God to give you His plan for your life and discover the signature mark that God has commissioned you to impact the world with ---next, intentionally take time to meditate, by saying to yourself who God has created you to be and what he has given you to accomplish. Meditate on being successful in what you believe God has called you to do and be in the world. Further in the book as you read, you will see where I have written out some things that you can also incorporate into you meditation.

The next in the four steps to possess your purpose and impact the world with your signature mark is visualization. **Visualization** is to form a mental image of something or someplace, it is also to imagine with the use of visual aid. This visualization should occur both intangibly and tangibly. It should occur intangibly through the use of your imagination and then be tangibly arranged on a vision board, thereby keeping the vision in front of you. The vision board serves as your 3-demensional touch-point of where you are going. Now, subconsciously through your consistent positive self-talk (meditation) and the tangible stimulus with your natural senses (visualization) being engaged, you are building this new image at your subconscious (invisible) level. You have got to embody what you desire and see yourself doing it. This may even mean changing your wardrobe to fit the image that you see on the inside of you. Socially, begin to surround yourself with those who are successful at doing what you desire to do. Begin to physically go to places where you see yourself going as you move into fulfilling your unique purpose. All of these visually stimulating experience work together to position you to transition comfortably into your unique purpose and as you continue in this you will develop your own unique signature mark.

The subconscious is to humans what the hard drive is to the modern day computer. It stores all of our memories, experiences, values, beliefs, conditionings and sensory experiences. These all culminate to comprise the way we live our lives, our world view and the basis by which we process and make our decisions.

In order for the effects of your impact of purpose to be measured, they must be seen. This brings us to the third key to possessing your purpose, which is demonstration.

**Demonstration** means to prove or show by evidence. This will require you to begin to act out your purpose and seek opportunities to exercise your unique abilities and gifts. By faith, your capacity to believe and manifest, you will now begin to attract the image that you have built on the inside of you, through meditation and visualization.

Take note as you begin to see this in your life, know that it is not a coincidence, this is how the Law of Faith works! Faith is the substance of things you hope for and the evidence of the things you cannot tangibly see in your current natural environment. As this process unfolds in your life it is critical that you exercise patience in your life. Patience can be described as consistently remaining consistent. That means that you do not become anxious and impatient, if it seems as though you are not progressing for a moment. You must continue to do what you know you are supposed to do to get where you need to be in spite of what your natural environment is displaying. The force of faith is at work and as you apply tangible action to your faith, you begin to see what you have believed for come into existence.

A simple illustration of this could be someone's desire to lose weight and exenterate their muscular tone. At first glance it could appear that no weight has been loss and no muscles have been toned, after one week, but if the correct diet and exercise are consistently performed, then after three, four, six and even eight weeks pass, the desired result begins to manifest and the patient endurance of eight consistent weeks eventually pay off.

It's not the short run but the long haul that gets the job done many times.

The fourth and final key for you to possess your purpose, is manifestation, which is the actualization of you fully carrying-out your purpose and doing what you were born into the earth to do! **Manifestation** is an indication of the existence or presence of something. The tangible expression of the expectation of a specific belief and an act of faith on behalf of an individual. To put it simply, it is to make the dreams and desires of your heart become your reality ---transforming your imagination into your reality, today.

**IMPACTING WITH YOUR PURPOSE**

Now that you have discovered how to possess your purpose, in this next section, you will learn how to effectively impact your world with your unique purpose. Impacting your world is basically to have an effect on it by leaving your lasting impression or signature mark on everything and with everyone you touch. By definition impact means to strike forcefully, to have an effect, the power of making a strong and immediate impression and the effect or impression of one thing on another. Based on those definitions of impact one could take away the fact that impacting is quite forceful and lasting. Ask yourself, what effect am I having in my world and how has that effect affected those around me?

It is interesting to note that throughout the world there are many people representing all cultures, nationalities and walks of life that have discovered their unique purpose but they do not go any further than simply knowing of it or having some idea of what they should be doing concerning it. They are content in simply being aware that they have unique abilities that could be used, but they never move to act on their unique abilities. Instead they have somehow become complacent and never chose to do anything about living out their unique purpose.

There is a story I told earlier in the book that gives reference to such individuals. This story was concerning the gentleman that was given an investment valued at about two year's wages, based on the economy of the time in which he lived. Sadly, he never got a return on the investment of money given to him but what's worse; he never even attempted to put that investment he received to work. He simply buried it and let it die. To allow the gifts and abilities that you were born with to die inside of you is not only unfortunate, but is an act of irresponsibility of the abilities that were freely given to you. This irresponsible act of neglect of the unique abilities given to an individual, results into a void in the fabric of our society. What I mean by void in the fabric of our society is, the songs that were never written, the art that was never drawn, the businesses that were never started, the government that was not guided correctly, the answer to problems that were never provided and all the ability, potential and solutions that were never released.

How many people in the world today are aware of their unique purpose or have some idea of the things and people that they should be affecting but have not yet stepped out on these great ideas to impact their world? Is it because of fear, laziness or flat out rebellion? Could it be that some people are rebelling against what they know that they should be doing? Obviously, these questions are for those individuals to answer because only they know the answer. It is the responsibility of us all to discover and work to fulfill our unique purpose. These are the questions that we must ask and challenge ourselves with daily.

I am here to inspire, motivate and encourage you to step out and begin to impact your world with your unique purpose. Your purpose is a gift, a specific unique investment given to you by God! He will not take it back, even if

*"It is the responsibility of us all to discover and work to fulfill our unique purpose."*

you do not put it to work. It is your responsibility to work it out and produce a profit from it. The profit from your unique purpose being invested is measured by the great increase that results in the lives of others based on your specific contribution to them and to the world at-large.

Impacting with your purpose is primarily done through the relationships you currently have and those that you seek to establish. The relationships you have are great intangible assets that must be cultivated and maintained to be most productive and fruitful. The words you say and the deeds you do all contribute to impacting the lives of others. Your relationships are key and contain within them the ability to make room for you in strategic places, provide preferential treatment, grant request, change legislations and influence cultures. Through the agency of networking and collaborating we begin to discover how important and meaningful relationships are to us. Be it direct or indirect, we all are in relationship with each other in some way and our purposes have an impact on the world we live in today. Manage your relationships wisely and do not be irresponsible with the friendships you make. Value those around you and put your purpose to work! Putting your purpose to work will enrich the lives of others as well as produce a profit for you.

*"Putting your purpose to work will enrich the lives of others as well as produce a profit for you."*

Here are some tangible real life examples of ways people can impact with their purpose. If your purpose is to lead in some capacity, then do it diligently and prudently because the decisions you make will impact those who you oversee. If your purpose is to speak out on an issue or on behalf of a particular cause do it with all conviction and the faith you have for it. If supporting someone in any specific way is your purpose, do it gladly with the ability you possess. Teach with great clarity, understanding and patience, if teaching is your purpose. As one who builds, do it with passion and skill. Those who innovate and create, share your work with generosity, making great strides in advancements that contribute to our collective increase. Advocates, who stand in the gap with justice as their cause, do it with all sincerity and truth.

Seek to impact your world with your unique purpose and you will be affecting the world as a whole in your service and contribution to others!

# CHAPTER 3

∞

## Unveiling the Identity of Your Unique Purpose

*I will praise thee; for I am fearfully and wonderfully made: marvellous are thy works; and that my soul knoweth right well.-Psalms 139:14 KJV*

## WHAT IS IMAGE?

Throughout the first two chapters we have discovered what purpose is and its expression in our lives. In these next several chapters we will explore what image is and its profound impact on our lives and purpose. We will cover the essentially important role it plays in our development, the embodiment of the unique purpose we contribute to those we serve and the significance of identifying our signature mark.

So, what is image? Image is the picture of our life that we live out each day. Image is who we are at our core. Image is something that is constantly under construction and that requires regular maintenance upkeep and updating. Image is conceived in our imagination, deposited into our subconscious mind, birthed with our words and solidified with our actions and behaviors. There is a lot to be said about image and how the images we have of ourselves shape our world. This image that we carry impacts the places we go, the people we meet, the opportunities we are presented with, the decisions we make and the things that we take ownership possession over in life.

People will go great lengths to fit the mold of the image they carry in their minds. On a global scale people spend billions each year in building an image that they would like to display to the world. There is a direct correlation between the image we have of ourselves and the fulfillment of our unique purpose. If there is a disconnect between the image we carry and our unique purpose then our purpose is placed in jeopardy and our destiny is then at stake.

We must see ourselves as a total and complete fulfillment of our unique purpose before destiny can be actualized. Seeing is not always believing, because what we see is subject to change but if you can believe a reality that you do not currently see existing before you, you can then cause what you currently see naturally existing before you to come into alignment with your belief. The way this works is that as you believe, you are beginning to embody and personify your belief and as you do this you also begin to attract to yourself the right and ideal opportunities to accomplish what you are believing for or to become. So think big and keep before you images that speak of your purpose and great destiny!

Where do we get these images from? They are conceived in our imagination through the things we hear, the things we see, our experiences and the way we have been conditioned from our youthful up-bringing. Have you ever thought about what makes successful people, successful or what sets apart the above average from the average? Why some thrive and always appear to be happy and content while some others fail and often seem to have a negative pessimistic view of life? It is nothing more than how they see themselves. This is known as self-image. It is the image that we have adopted as our own that we exhibit before people on a daily basis. This image is used to define who we are and where we are going. Think about this, when you set out to go to a particular place or do a specific thing, you must first see it in your mind and envision completing it before you ever start it. It is upon completion in your mind that you begin and follow through to the set destination.

No one on this earth does anything without first seeing it in their imagination. I believe it is impossible to do anything without first seeing it in your mind as done and completed. The images we have are pictures and those pictures are formed primarily from words or external images in our immediate environment. We then internalize these images and begin to act them out as if it we

> *"No one on this earth does anything without first seeing it in their imagination."*

were involved in a stage production. At first, if these images contradict what we believe, it will feel awkward and foreign. If no maintenance is applied to this new belief system and pattern of behavior we reject it and revert back to the comfort and safety of the old images and belief system that we previously knew and were acquainted.

Distorted images are those images that have been altered or manipulated from the correct or genuine origin of one's purposeful intent, often due to poor models demonstrated before an individual as they have grown and developed throughout their life. In cases of distorted images there must be correction and changes made from within the person, this begins with the thinking and perception that a person holds of them self. Changing your image is a lot like an actor preparing for a new role and getting into "character". The more acquainted he or she becomes with the new scene, new script, new conversations, different responses and newly adopted behaviors, the more the new image of the character emerges. It is at this point that the signature mark of an individual is developed and shaped.

Ask yourself, '…in my life, are there distorted images that need correcting?' Is my image aligned with the purpose of my life? Is it time for me to re-image and re-align my life with the image of my purpose? My friend, if the answer is yes, then begin today to think positive thoughts concerning you and your worth and value as a person, then begin to align your conversation to that which is in line with your unique purpose. You must ask God to reveal to you who He has created you to be and what he desires for you to accomplish.

God has prepared you as a master workmanship and a unique one-of-a-kind, in the book of Ephesians 2:10, it reads, "For we are His workmanship, created in Christ Jesus unto good works, which God hath before ordained that we should walk in them."(KJV) We have been chosen, selected and hand-picked by the Lord, which by itself should be enough to bolster your esteem, that God, the creator of all things has personally selected you to do a specific work for Him. He has intricately designed you to be the unique person that you are

> *"God has prepared you as a master workmanship and a unique one-of-a-kind."*

and He has given you your own signature mark to be a part of His plan in the earth. You are accepted and are especially special to God who created you. You are made in His image and after His likeness (Genesis 1:26-27). You were born with purpose in mind. God thinks highly of you and knows your beginning from your end. He took His time when planning and mapping out your life; He has made you to be an answer to someone else's problem or to be the solution for world oppressing issues.

Jeremiah 29:11 says, For I know the thoughts that I think toward you, saith the LORD, thoughts of peace, and not of evil, to give you an expected end."(KJV) God has prepared an expected positive destiny for you! Consume your thoughts with what God's word says concerning you and not the negative images and conversations that are inundating society today. Remember you are always led in the direction of your most dominant thought. What new image will you adopt as your own for yourself?

*"Remember you are always led in the direction of your most dominant thought."*

As the saying goes, 'you are what you eat', so it is with image, you will become what you consume in abundance. The things that you feed on, or think about the most have a tremendous impact in not only who you become by those thoughts, but where you go in life and how effective you are at impacting the world with your unique God given purpose and signature mark.

Discontinue all negative and counter-productive relationships. Refrain from listening to things that establishes and builds unhealthy images of you. Become disciplined at what you allow to come from your mouth during the conversations you engage. Understanding that our image is built by the words we hear and speak, the things we consistently watch and look at, the thoughts we entertain and adopt as our own, our social conditioning and the teachings and values we have embraced and allowed as authorities in our life. Those afore mentioned things are the primary basis and foundation of how our images are formed and how image is constructed in our lives. They represent the framework of how an individual see themselves. Let me ask you , how do you desire to be seen? Where do you desire to go in life? What impact do you desire to have on society? When will you begin to build the image that you desire to be? Now is the time and today is the day!

**WHY IS IMAGE IMPORTANT?**

Why is image important? I have heard it said that if purpose is not known, abuse is inevitable. This statement means that without a correct image, that is, an image that is distorted, one's purpose is not recognized or utilized. Anyone who is does not comprehend or is unaware of their unique purpose, places their destiny in jeopardy because they are not living or functioning for the purpose of their existence. Understand that you can't go where you cannot see. Your purpose illuminates your image and your purpose is fueled by the core passion of your heart. Image is immensely important in the actualizing of your purpose and in attaining your destiny. You may have heard the story of the eagle that was hatched in the chicken coop; in this story there was an eagle egg that somehow found its way inside a chicken coop. As is the custom of incubation for most foul, the mother hen discovered the egg and sat on it to protect it and to continue the incubation process.

As time passed the egg eventually cracked and behold, an eagle was born. The mother hen cared for the baby eaglet as if it were her own. During the course of the eagle's development, he observed the fact that the other chickens had wings but seldom if ever used them. He often wondered why the others around him never flew or even talked about flying. He noticed that when they were fed, they ate off of the ground as their food was thrown at them. Inside he never felt right about food being thrown at him and eating it off the ground or being hand fed by someone else. Inside, his innate eagle image was being distorted and the image of a high flying eagle was diminishing.

While living life as a chicken he never ever truly felt that he fit in or that he was a part of the chicken class. Those around him noticed that he did not look like them and that he was much larger than them. His desire was to fly high and soar as high as the mountain tops in the clouds. From time to time he would see other eagles soaring high and something inside of him would instantly identify with them. Because he never used his wings they became nearly useless to him, but one day while none of the chicken's were around he ran across a piece of broken glass on the ground and saw his reflection in it. He noticed that he resembled those "high flying" eagles that he saw occasionally from time to time.

As days went by he began to make other discoveries and the more discoveries he made the greater the distinction became between he and the chicken's all around him. He noticed that he ran faster, ate more and had larger wings that when flapped lifted him off the ground. More days passed and with all the discoveries he made, a new image was being built. This new image shifted his passion and desire to hang around with the chicken's to desiring to be with birds that flew high. This new image of himself changed his conversation from "ground-level" talk to "high-flying" cloud soaring talk, he now used the wings that for so long he never used and they began to be strengthened. His appetite changed and his hunger deepened, all of a sudden he was not satisfied with the rationed hand-outs given to him and was certainly not appreciative of the fact that they were thrown at him.

He had a sense that he was made for flying and that the high skies were his domain. This new image had made this once, chicken-minded, ground-level talking, confused bird into a disciplined and focused, purpose-driven, high-flying eagle. So one day when no other chicken's were around the eagle decided he would put these new discoveries to the test, he ran and ran as fast as he could and with a belief in his heart and hope in his eyes he spread his wings and off he went. A gust of wind propelled him upward and before he realized it, his feet were not on the ground and the chicken coop below him became as a distant memory as he gained more and more height into the clouds he soared.

What could we learn from this story? Amongst the top prevailing lessons, we discovered that with a new and correct image one will do more and be more than he or she ever believed possible for them. I will say it again; you can't go where you cannot see. The right image must be in you, in order to fulfill your unique purpose.

As this new image is being built you will begin to notice that everything around you begins to change as a result of the change

> *"The right image must be in you in order for you to fulfill your unique purpose."*

that is occurring on the inside of you! Those whom you associate with and become friends with are in direct correlation to the new image of who you are becoming. The effect of the new way that you see yourself is drawing to you all the resources you will need to be successful in your unique purpose.

The way that you see yourself is the way that you will be seen and interpreted by others. Your values, interests and perspectives change as you change and their reflections are made evident by the decisions you make and the company you keep. You have heard it said that your network will determine your net worth. This merits some value, because the relationships you invest in now will yield a harvest for you later. Those who see you and have identified you in the past by the old incorrect and distorted image you once exemplified, will began to say, "what happened to him" or "who does she thing she is", as they do this remain steadfast in the new you and you will discover yourself in the right places at the right times with all the right information required to be successful in your unique purpose. The unique purpose that only you can fulfill, the signature you!

Your conversation and attitude will change as you build this new image inside you as seen in the case of the eagle, as he made new discoveries about himself, his world changed and so will your world change with the new image you build inside of you. He no longer talked about low-level issues and the woes of the here and now but he thought on a higher level and spoke on greater aspirations and of better things to come. He realized that he was of value and he gained a sense of dignity so much so that he no longer appreciated the fact that his food was thrown at him. As you build the new image of who you really are and were created to be you will gain a sense of dignity as well and you will not stand for just anything that is thrown at you, in your life, but you will learn to appreciate the best and develop an appetite for things of great quality.

*"You were born for a specific purpose and your reason for being is incredibly significant."*

Image is important because with it you began to embrace a greater appreciation for the gifts, abilities and skills you possess. You discover why you are good at what you are good at and how your unique abilities fit into your unique purpose. The right image is an essential factor in the overall discovery, development and achievement of your unique purpose and living your signature life.

I am excited and passionate about this topic concerning how your image is linked to your destiny and how you can live you signature life! You were born for a specific purpose and your reason for being is incredibly significant. The purpose that you were born for, will take you places and connect you with people that you may not have ever traveled to or had an acquaintance in meeting, had you not discovered, embraced and lived out your unique purpose. Your destiny which is the result of your unique purpose would not be attainable without first building and maintaining the correct image.

## THE FRUSTRATED OFFICER

Suppose a police officer were to prepare for work one day as a street intersection traffic-controller but while preparing to dress up for work that day he put on his favorite sports team jersey over his uniform top with his badge attached to it and wore the matching cap with it.

As he approached his post and took his place in the middle of the busy intersection people began to blow their horns and shout obscenities at him. With traffic mounting and the continued negative comments being shouted at him he became frustrated at the lack of respect, chaotic traffic situation and the feeling of being out of control and out of place. Hours passed and now it was lunch time, during his lunch, the officer took off the sports team jersey and placed his police hat on his head.

Returning from lunch, the officer again took his post and resumed directing traffic but this time the drivers obeyed his directives and some even replied, 'thank you officer' and 'may I proceed now, sir'. This stark contrast in attitude and behavior of the motorists caused the officer to reflect on the events of his morning. Thinking back he realized that being out of uniform had an overwhelming impact on the first half of his day. For starters, he could not effectively manage the traffic, he also received no respect as an officer of the law and lastly he began to feel frustrated and totally out of control as well as out of place.

Keeping this story in mind, we know that ordinarily this occurrence probably never happens, but let's analyze this story to take away some lessons that apply to discovering why image is important and how image is linked to fulfilling our destiny and living our signature life.

Image is the fabric of our lives. If you are operating with a distorted image, you are placing your destiny at serious risk as well as cheating the people you are assigned to help in life. Knowing who you are and operating in the unique purpose and capacity that you were designed to fulfill, will take you to the places that cross the paths of the people to do the things and solve the problems you were meant to solve and accomplish. I know that sounds like a lot, but what I am saying is that to complete the course of your God ordained destiny you must play the part, playing the part requires building and maintaining the correct image inside of you to do what you have been birthed to do.

In the case of the police officer suffering from the lack of a correct image, his ordained and destined environment rejected him leaving him with feelings of frustration, being out of place and a sense of inadequacy because he was not identified as a police officer by those around him. Understand that it is solely your responsibility to develop and maintenance your image. If you are operating in a role or doing a particular task you feel as though you cannot do or you feel like you are not performing it as proficiently as you may like to, then reflect on the task and

*"Image is the fabric of our lives."*

identify exactly what you believe it takes to master it then began to build your image-capacity to undertake the task at a mastering level. This is image building 101. Understand that image is the revelation or unveiling of who you really are, it reveals your signature mark to the world. With the correct image of who you are in place, you are confident, bold and courageous. Image is the picture of our life that we live out each day.

Image is who we are at our core. The thoughts we have of ourselves and the level or degree to which we esteem ourselves are developed in our imagination and they form pictures, these pictures are emulated by us in our daily interactions. We strive to be like and model ourselves after those pictures produced in our imagination. That emulation and imitation process becomes the image that we have of ourselves and thereby limit us to where and how far we go in life, more particularly how well we fulfill our unique purpose. In the course of us fulfilling our specific unique purpose we meet and are acquainted with our bright destinies and experience signature living.

Our destiny is the accomplishment of the unique purpose we serve and our unique purpose is the accomplishment of the correct image of who we are inside of us. Simply put, our destiny is shaped by and directly related to the image we possess. Our image is the unveiling of our imagination to the world.

## GENERATIONAL LEADERSHIP

*"We shape our world through our imagination and the words we say."*

If you can see it, you can be it. This is good news! Good news for every person in every country of the world! We have the opportunity to be whatever we want to be, go wherever we desire to go and do whatever it is we desire to do in life. We shape our world through our imagination and the words we say. I have heard it said that, your feet will never go where your mind has never been. This is true and is something that a lot of people in the world have never mastered, the positive use of their imagination and intentional positive self-talk.

51

There is a story of an ancient generation of people that missed out on their inheritance due to the negative use of their imagination and the poor choice of words that they spoke and believed. There were only two leaders from this entire generation of nearly three and a half million people that enjoyed their inheritance. They did not succumb to the negative and defeated self-perception of those around them. They constantly engaged in positive self-talk and imagined themselves to be well-able to take possession of their inheritance that had been laid up and made available to them.

You have a bright future and you may not even know it. Take time to discover your gifts and talents. As you make these discoveries, invest the time required in becoming good at them and mastering them. These gifts and talents will make room for you among the great and most of all be used to serve those you are assigned to and solve problems that are perplexing the world.

*"You have a bright future and you may not even know it."*

Your *destiny* is the relationships, places and stages that you transitions to as a result of you fulfilling your unique purpose and living your signature life!

Your *purpose* is the original intent and plan by design of God, the creator and manufacturer of all people, places and things!

Your *image* is the picture or idea you possess of yourself as projected to the world!

*"Purpose is the original intent by design of a creator or manufacturer of any person, place or thing!"*

In the Bible, there was a man named Joseph, the son of Jacob, who God renamed, Israel. Joseph's rise to prominence was directly related to his healthy image of himself.

He was hated and ridiculed by his own brothers, kidnapped by his brothers, sold into slavery, thrown into prison, but eventually went on to be appointed prime minister of Egypt and thereby used instrumentally to become a major strategist and governmental leader in the known world at that time. This would not have been possible had Joseph not had a positive image of himself through-out all of his perils and trials. At an early age God gave him a dream that he would one day be a ruler and that image of rulership stuck with him. This image carried him from his small hometown to leading one of the most powerful nations and economies in the known world at that time. If this happened for Joseph it can happen for you!

## EMANCIPATED BY IMAGE

On January 1, 1863, President Abraham Lincoln signed the Emancipation Proclamation. This enacted an order that all slaves in every territory be freed from the bondage of their slave masters. About 4 million descendants of disenfranchised African slaves gained freedom as a result of this famous legal document. President Lincoln recognized that all men were created equal and that everyone should live with dignity, purpose and freedom. He understood what life was like to live under the bondage and oppression of poverty as well the joys that come as a result of liberty. On November 19, 1863, during the Gettysburg Address, President Lincoln said, "Four score and seven years ago our fathers brought forth on this continent, a new nation, conceived in Liberty, and dedicated to the proposition that all men are created equal." It was his belief that all men were created equal and that without freedom a man has no identity. Being free and having the right and opportunity to express who you were created to be is important. He understood image and its immense value in the lives of every human being. Image had a lot to do with the many successes of President Lincoln, and although he experienced many setbacks and failures he never quit because he understood that God had created him to do something great.

During President Lincoln's life, he overcame an impoverished early life, he was demoted from Capitan to Private in the Illinois militia, self-taught himself to become a lawyer, rejected and humiliated by his attorney peers, ran for IL state representative six times, for US representative once, for Senate twice, defeated for Vice Presidency nomination, but went on to win the Presidency of the United States of America in 1860 and again in 1864. The image he had of himself far overshadowed the many perils and calamities he endured. He had a sense of the tremendous value that God had placed inside of him. His extensive political career spanned from 1832 until 1864, during this thirty-two year time period, his name showed up on nine electoral ballots and through every loss he got back up and continued to move forward towards the goals he set out to achieve.

He had the image of a victorious champion and nothing would be able to stop or hold him back from successfully accomplishing and actualizing how he saw himself and nothing should be able to stop you either. You have to see yourself winning in life ---you must view yourself as the victor and not the victim!

*"You must view yourself as the victor and not the victim!"*

You have to decide today that you are special and that God has created you to be great and do great things and that you were born for such a time as this, to be a problem solver and a solution maker. You determine your script. Your image is the link to you fulfilling your destiny!

# CHAPTER 4

∞

## Releasing Your Signature Mark

**Before I formed thee in the belly I knew thee; and before thou camest forth out of the womb I sanctified thee, and I ordained thee a prophet unto the nations.** *-Jeremiah 1:5 KJV*

## YOU ARE MARVOLOUSLY MADE

Everyone born into the earth has a unique and specific destiny and divine design. Sad thing is that many people never realize this and for some that do, it is well beyond their youthful years. God has assignments for each of us to

> *"Everyone born into the earth has a unique and specific destiny and divine design."*

fulfill but getting caught up in the hustle bustle routine of "trying to make it" has caused much of the world to place their unique gifting and talents down by the way-side of life in exchange for a job or unrelated work opportunities that are not at all linked to fulfilling their purpose or reaching their God ordained destinies. Life, in many people's eyes is viewed as a mere survival existence. It is important to take a greater view of your life and ask yourself, what legacy will I leave after I am gone? What do I desire to be known for? What impact or mark will I leave? It is only when you change the way you see things, that the things you see change. You must see your life as more than just a series of unrelated events. Life must become meaningful to you!

*"You must see your life as more than just a series of unrelated events."*

There was a 30-year case study performed from January 1, 1973 until December 31, 2003, this study involved three age groups of retiree's. The first cohort group of retiree's was age 55 and the second group was in their 60's. The case study was observed by a group of researchers that reviewed the survival outcomes of 839 employees who retired at age 55 and 1,929

58

employees who retired at age 60 and were still alive by the time they reached age 65. These outcomes were compared with a third group of 900 employees who retired at 65. Women made up only about 11% of the total study population. The results that the researchers reported of this study showed that 137 workers who retired at age 55 died by age 65, in contrast, 98 workers who retired at age 60 died by age 65. After adjusting on the basis of gender, the year the participants joined the study, and socioeconomic status, the researchers concluded that those of higher socioeconomic status appeared to be permitted to retire earlier.

The point of this case study was to observe the age at which people retired from a job or career and the long term survival rate of that industrial population. What this study revealed was that those who retired early at age 55 had almost double the mortality risk than those who retired in their 60's. In fact, those who retired at age 55 in the high socioeconomic status category had a 20% greater risk of dying, according to the study and those in the low socioeconomic status category that retired by 55 years olds had nearly a 60% increased mortality risk. Why was this? Could it be that those who retired early at age 55 never discovered their unique purpose and signature mark, could it be that they believed they had nothing more to live for, or perhaps they had nothing else to contribute to life. Did they lose their perspective on life? Obviously, there were other contributing factors that led to the demise of various members of the cohort groups but one question that could apparently be taken away from this study of those who retired early would be, 'you retired from your jobs and careers to engage in what?' This is the million dollar question. Was the job that they retired from all that they were living for? Did they see a future for themselves outside of the job? Was there a life for them after the job? Did they lose meaning and purpose for living, once they retired?

The way you view your life is the way you live your life. Will you live your life purposefully and with intentionality or will all of your days amount to an unrelated and aimless existence? Remember, if purpose is not known abuse is inevitable. You are marvelously made in the sight

> *"The way you view your life is the way you live your life."*

of God and are of incomparable value to His plan for humanity in your world and in the world around you. Unfortunately, we see that when people do not recognize their unique purpose they suffer from low self-esteem and an inferiority complex, they often have little expectation for their own lives and futures. They operate under low-ceilings and seldom ever experience upward mobility.

This is primarily why our young people are killing one-another at alarming rates, or why Americans are feeding themselves to death, and why fifty-percent of marriages in the United States end in divorce. People have not discovered purpose.

As I defined earlier in the book, purpose is the original intent by design of a creator or manufacturer of any person place or thing. Learn to love you! You must love who you are and celebrate your giftings and talents. Your purpose in life serves as a navigation tool to guide you to your destiny. Without purpose one is as a ship out to sea without a course tossed to and fro aimlessly. Without purpose you have no destination. Think about it, if you don't know where you are going in life, any road will get you there. Your destiny is defined by your purpose and your purpose is captured in your giftings. This is what I mean by that statement ---the giftings that we possess are like a seed, which stores the DNA, capacity and potential for us to become and accomplish whatever we are designed to produce in our life. Another way to look at it is like, the giftings we possess are the tools we need to do whatever it is we are to do in life.

Our purpose is the product, that is, the result of us working with the gifts we were given. Our destiny is the result of the purpose we were designed and born to fulfill. The people and places that were impacted by our touch; those whose lives will be forever changed, positively, by the impression of our signature mark left on them.

For instance, if someone has a gift to sing and they work hard at mastering this gift, then eventually they arise to a place of prominence and their music is impacting people positively all around the world. Now, let's say that with the money they made during their music career they go on to do humanitarian works that save the lives of thousands of starving children or provide needed resources to those without clean running water or they build schools and pay for teachers to educate the uneducated. This is purpose in action and the relationships, places and stages that you transition through as a result of you performing your unique purpose is called destiny. When you perform your purpose you do it in a way that only you can do it, which is your signature mark on it. This is the beauty of living on purpose. You begin to embody the purpose that you are living; this is your passion for life. Your purpose is fueled by the burning desire you have on the inside of you to be all that you were born to be and live your best life...your signature life!

**TRANSFORMED THINKING**

To live your signature life, you must first change the way you view your life, this begins in your mind. You must first rid yourself of what are known as mind viruses. A mind virus is a mental stagnation, a resistance to change often manifesting as excuses in a person's life. If things are not working out according as you planned, do not automatically blame some external factor as the cause and allow that to become your excuse for not accomplishing your goal. Instead, it is important to first take inventory of what you really believe and see if it may be something in you that is causing you not to succeed.

All of this begins in our minds, more specifically our subconscious mind where 88 to 90 percent of our behavior is derived from. What we believe, we do. Our beliefs shape our perceptions; our perceptions begin to then shape our reality. What do you believe about yourself? How do you perceive yourself? Who do you think you are? For as a man thinks in his heart, so is he. You will become what you believe and in life, you will end up exactly at the level of your belief. If you believe that you will accomplish a thing, you will, but if you believe you will not accomplish a thing, you will not. You decide how far you will go in life, how much you will achieve, how rich you will be and where you will go. These are all up to you and they rest in your ability to make a decision. The responsibility is yours and yours alone, no one can stop you from reaching your destiny but you!

The way you think will change your life. Your thoughts impact your perceptions. Your perceptions impact your behavior. Your behaviors form habits. These habits impact your outcomes. The outcomes you experience in life are a result of the way that you think of yourself and the direction you are headed in life!

Here is a classic example of the impact that your thinking has on your outcomes. Let's use healthy choices in how a person eats.

*"You're always led in the direction of your most dominant thought."*

Their thoughts toward eating right impact their perception of fruits and vegetables positively. This positive perception of fruits and vegetables impacts their behaviors causing them to consume them at a greater frequency. This behavior leads to a habit of eating right. The healthy eating habits have an impact on the outcome of that person's life and physical health. That was a simple illustration, but it is applicable for anything a person desires to achieve in life.

Here is a Statement: You're always led in the direction of your most dominant thought. What are the thoughts you have concerning your life?

Let me tell you, You are God's masterpiece!!! You are a one-of-a-kind, there has never been, neither will there ever be another you. You have been uniquely designed to do whatever it is that you were born to do. You must discipline your mind and train yourself to think positively about who you are and your purpose in life. In Philippians 4:8 the scripture tells us to think on whatever is ***true, right, honest, just, pure, lovely, excellent, of good report, praise worthy*** ... think on these things.

You are a product of your thought life!!! God himself calls you his masterpiece in Scripture... Ephesians 2:10 (NLT), "For we are God's Masterpiece. He has created us anew in Christ Jesus, so we could do the good things He planned for us long ago." Now that you know that you are God's masterpiece it is time for you to go further and discover your purpose and signature mark as a one-of-a-kind masterpiece!

View it as if everyone in the world has their own uniquely shaped puzzle piece and that piece is a part of a large puzzle. Every day that you are given, to live, you hold that piece in your hands in the form of your unique abilities, gifting and talents, which your purpose is inextricably attached too. The piece you have in your hand represents your purpose or contribution to the whole entire puzzle in this illustration. Without your piece the puzzle cannot be completed. Your purpose matters greatly and you are tremendously significant! You have a unique purpose and when God created you he knew there would be problems to solve and with those problems he had you in mind to solve them. Someone is counting on you to discover your unique purpose, fulfill it and leave your signature mark!!!

The scripture tells us that people are destroyed for lack of knowledge (Hosea 4:6). Knowledge of your purpose is critical to you successfully achieving your God ordained destiny. Remember, if purpose is not known, abuse is in evitable. Others are waiting on you to live out your purpose and make your signature mark on the world. Only you can do it ---in your family, at work, in the community, in the city, in the nation, and in the world!!!

**THE DECREE TO DOMINATE**

In Genesis 1:28, scripture tells us that God blessed man and gave him dominion over his works on earth. Again in Psalms 8:6 it says, "Thou madest him to have dominion over the works of thy hands; thou hast put all things under his feet:"(KJV)  In Genesis 2:15 God gave Adam a specific assignment within this command to dominate ---it was to care for and tend to the Garden of Eden.

What is your garden to care for and tend to? What or who are you motivated to service in life? Where do your passions lie? Many times in life those things that we are most passionate about are indications of where our purpose is suited to be fulfilled. When talking about purpose it is important to remember that it is not an all of a sudden thing. It's like that illustration of the seed I talked about earlier in the book, it will start small, but as you care for it and tend to it and work hard at developing it, it will bud and blossom and grow.

Everything that God gives to us, he gives it to us in seed form. God desires for us to rule and dominate through our purpose by the endowment of gifts he has given us. You were not gifted for your gifts to lie dormant inside of you and not produce a product; it was for God's purpose and glory that you have been gifted! When others see you thriving in your gift, God gets the glory. So, identify what you do best and effortlessly. Look for clues, signals and indicators; these are evident in many instances by our passions and desires. Pursue your passion and learn to articulate your purpose in your conversation. Once you master how to articulate your purpose; now you will begin to attract to yourself the resources you need to meet and accomplish your goals!

Here are some indicators and insights that will clue you into the seed of purpose that God has sown in you!

Natural Ability

Passionate Interest

Discoveries / Occurrences

## Natural Ability

Natural abilities are those things that you seem to do effortlessly, these things come to you naturally and you perform them well. You've heard it before, 'he's a natural or she's a natural...' These are things that you received no formal training or schooling for, you just do them well.

## Passionate Interest

Passionate interests are those things that peak your interest. These are the things that you may not know much about but you have a strong desire and passion to discover and master them. Some examples of this could be a person's interest in technology, business, government, healthcare, science, performing arts or... you fill in the blank.

## Discoveries / Occurrences

Discoveries and occurrences are things you are already engaged in but it has not occurred to you that this is a part or connected to you operating in your purpose. These are commonly called "aha-moments"

It is up to you to water and cultivate the seed giftings you have been given, by sharpening, refining, researching, getting training, being mentored and getting coaching in the areas that you are passionate about and that intersect with your predominant giftings.

Skills are learned through training. Gifts are given to you from God. You must develop them from within you. God has given each one of us gifts. He expects us to dominate in our purpose through the use of our unique giftings.

## PERSONAL PROGRESS

Personal example, I have a gift to communicate and build others up, however, I had to develop my gifts of communicating and building others up, by acquiring skills such as public speaking skills, life coaching skills, counseling skills, business development skills, and team-building skills. The skills I acquired assist me in performing my purpose, they are used to accentuate and enhance my core giftings of communicating and building others up. As I continue to move ahead in my purpose and career, I must remain sharp and current with the skills that I have acquired.

Many times people whose gifts are apparent, and seem to come naturally, seldom think that they have to continue to work on improving them. Even the best and most talented athletes and entertainers must continuously train and practice to remain sharp and perform excellently.

If you are going to dominate in any area, sphere, industry or field, this implies that you are going to have to be on top and ahead. To dominate means that you have a commanding influence and that people are impressed, inspired out-run by your performance. This means that you are the standard and that your work sets the bar. At this level of success you must be confident in your ability, know who you are and always press to do better, go further and dig deeper. Dominate has a root word, that word is "do". This means in order to dominate you must first do something.

Sir Isaac Newton's first law of motion states, *"Every object in a state of uniform motion tends to remain in that state of motion unless an external force is applied to it."* So, this means that you must put into motion your purpose by working your giftings and talents. Nothing just happens. *"For every action there is an equal and opposite reaction,"* states Newton's third law of motion. This basically means that whatever you put into the process of developing your giftings and pursuing your purpose is what you will get out of that process of developing your giftings and pursuing your purpose. To increase your chances of winning in life and see the results of your signature mark in the world, you must master the principle of achievement, this principle states that it is the effort exerted and the direction traveled, not wishful thinking alone that will bring you to an expected end or desired destination. So, burst out of the box, come out of the cave and shatter the glass of your own comfort zone by stepping into the domain that God has prepared for you and taking dominion by doing what you are called and destined to achieve.

## KEYS TO LIVING ON PURPOSE

- Know your goals and be intimately acquainted with them.

- Make a list of them and always keep the big picture in mind.

- Meet your objectives by acting and being a doer.

- Be disciplined, determined, and dedicated.

- Be a person of integrity and live your life by a set of guidelines and principles.

- Be knowledgeable and excellent in all that you do.

- Be confident!

- Be compassionate and always remember that life is all about people and relationships.

- Never get the Big head because you do not know it all.

# CHAPTER 5

∞

## In Pursuit of Purpose

*For I reckon that the sufferings of this present time are not worthy to be compared with the glory which shall be revealed in us.*
*For the earnest expectation of the creature waiteth for the manifestation of the sons of God.*
*-Romans 8:18-19 KJV*

**CONTRIBUTING FACTOR**

The following chapters will serve as a guide for you in the pursuit of your unique purpose in life. They will lead you in the general direction of your giftings and strengths, allowing you the opportunity to discover and develop your unparalleled unique purpose for living your signature life.  You will be given the opportunity to freely discover the vision you have for your life and your call to action will be to then unveil to the world who you really are and what your unique purpose for living is, as well as become a contributing factor to the world-at-large in your own specific capacity. You have a contributing part to play in the advancement and progression of your world. You have a signature mark to release.

As you go through this book keep in mind that the discovery and implementation of your unique purpose and signature mark is a direct point of contact with reaching your destiny. Your destiny is basically where you end up in the course of history as it relates to the completion of your unique purpose.

> *"Destiny is the relationship, places and stages one transition's to through the course of their life as a result of them performing their unique purpose."*

I define destiny as the relationships, places and stages one transition's to through the course of their life as a result of them performing their unique purpose.

Arriving at your destiny is a summation of your contribution to society on a microcosmic level in your own personal sphere of influence or on a macrocosmic level, on a global scale and the journey that you have taken as a result of making those contributions.

So discovering your unique purpose is simply the commencement on your road to destiny. Be advised this is not a coincidental occurrence, it is in fact a deliberate and intentional series of discoveries and implementations that are constantly unfolding, it is not something that happens after reading one book or answering a battery of questions.

Make the discovery and implementation of your unique purpose a significant priority in your life. Purpose is the very essence and quality of life and your unique purpose is the point of your life. The weight, value and worth of your unique purpose are absolutely incomparable! Make your time spent going through these next few chapters a pleasurable and memorable time.

Enjoy the information found in the next few chapters and use it as reference material as you continue to develop and grow in pursuit of purpose. This book cannot tell you specifically your God given purpose; however, it can be used to point you in the general direction and serve as an indicator of where you may fit in the grand scheme of fulfilling your unique purpose.

Remember, you are an important contributing part of the future of the world as we know it!

## AN INTROSPECTIVE LOOK

Ask yourself the following questions, as you draw from your memory, go as deep into your memory bank as you can recall: After you have answered these questions take time to reflect on them.

**From my youth I can remember I enjoyed doing what the most?**

**Currently, in my life now I enjoy doing what the most?**

**What activities do I have most passion and energy doing?**

## AN INTROSPECTIVE LOOK

As a result of my tremendous enjoyment while doing this
_____, I find that I am also very satisfied and
extremely fulfilled in this activity?


What things in life seem to bother you the most and many
times call you to action to change them?


What is the foremost burning passion and desire on your
heart to do in life?


In your imagination what do you see yourself doing as a
part of your life-work?

## A COLLABORATIVE EXTERNAL LOOK

This next set of questions are meant to analyze you from a collaborative vantage point. Based on your experiences, what have others such as your spouse, sister, brother, mother, father, a cousin, an aunt, uncle or a close friend said about you regarding the following questions:

**What have others said comes natural to you?**

**What have others said, that you are good at doing?**

**What have others said, are dominant abilities that they have seen in your life?**

**What would others say is most important to you?**

**What activity would others say makes you the most happiest by doing?**

## A LOOK FROM YOUR OWN NATURAL ENVIRONMENT

These questions draw on general and specific experiences you have had in your own natural environment, your personal sphere of influence and in your world socially.

**Throughout your life, what thing do you recall people saying that you do well?**

**In your own opinion, what way have you contributed most in the lives of others?**

## A LOOK FROM YOUR OWN NATURAL ENVIRONMENT

**What seems to occur naturally with you?**

    *a.  People seem to follow me on ideas and projects*

    *b.  People many times seeks my advice on a matter*

    *c.  I always have ideas of how to improve on things I see*

    *d.  I seem to come up with feasible witty inventive things and methods*

    *e.  I do these particular things exceptionally well and almost effortlessly.  Take some time to **list them:***


**Traditionally, I am characterized as (what) _____ in my family and as (what) _____ with my friends?**


**What things do you enjoy participating as a volunteer?**

The purpose of our lives could be synonymous with the theme of our lives. It is important that we do not ignore the consistent patterns and re-emerging theme that our lives perpetuate.

It could be said that the sense of fulfillment and worth that is felt when performing a task or deed and the effortless accomplishments that transpire during our engagement in completing a project, all point to a strength and unique ability that we possess.

Keep in mind that all these exercises are geared to point you to a general area of unique ability and are thereby indicators of a purposeful capacity that you will serve well in and become a contributing player in your world and potentially one day, the world at large.

By answering the following questions below, discover in what capacity you were involved in a specific activity and felt true intrinsic fulfillment.

**When was the last time that you felt that your life was most meaningful?**

**What task(s) do you perform and feel as though you are being most helpful to others?**

**In what way do you express the best of yourself to others?**

**When engaged in what expression or activity do you feel happiest and most fulfilled?**

**What comes naturally and effortlessly to you?**

**What do others say comes naturally and effortlessly to you?**

**What do you do that brings absolute joy to your life?**

**Take time to create a list of the attributes that you would like to be known for.**

There is a common thread in each one of our lives that seem to connect the dots that lead us to discovering our purpose. The people we meet, the places we go, the things we like and enjoy, the situations we find ourselves in and even the challenges that we must overcome many times point us towards the general direction of our purpose. There is a re-emerging theme that will not go away and seems to be a constant source of drive and inspiration that moves us to do what we do best and serves as our motivation for life.

We see things in people and immediately have a kindred connection to those things in them that cause them to do what they do and we identify with them.

To really live your signature life and release your mark on your world, there are a few questions you should answer--- these questions are designed to assist you in discovering what inspires you the most and what may be your predominant place in life. Even though you may share a similar passion with someone else, you still have your own unique signature way, style and voice. An example of this could be the variety of talk shows, both past and present, they all were shows that invited guests and talked about trending issues of their day but each one had and currently has their own signature mark that distinguishes them.

You are the same way, you may do similar things like another but you have your own signature twist on it and no one can do it like you. Even nature has illustrated this to us, for example, in the winter season, in those places that get snow, each snowflake may appear to be identical to one another but upon closer observation, they are all uniquely and individually designed. As you see others doing what you have a passion for and may believe is a part of your purpose, it is important not to get jealous and definitely not to compare yourself. You are uniquely made and your unique purpose is incomparable. There is no need to compare or compete with anyone, you are unique and of indispensible value, keep this in mind as you answer the following questions.

> *"You are uniquely made and your unique purpose is incomparable."*

Your answers to the following questions will be yet another lead for you in learning more about yourself, as you discover your purpose and live your signature life. As you read through the questions, take note of your motive and the reason behind the answers you come up with.

Here we go ---when talking about purpose you cannot avoid talking about vision because the two are related, currently what vision do you have for your life?

The vision you have serves as a guide for you in life as you meet goals and attain success. Often times we see other people performing in life and can identify with what they are doing, it's like something inside of us gets excited and we say, "I can see myself doing that…" So, who are some people you admire and what inspires you about them? As history is made each day, we should be learning more and more. Who were some people in history that inspired you and why?

## THE NEW YOU

Now that you have begun to identify yourself by many of the attributes that you currently possess and that you may see in others, begin to intentionally conduct yourself in a way that accentuates these attributes. Allow the list of questions that you have answered to epitomize you and as you do, others will begin to recognize you by those answers and the list of attributes that you provided. This subtle recognition will now begin to become your identity and you will become know for and identified by the behavior you exhibit ---these lifestyle habits you have adopted will also began to impact the decisions you make in a positive way.

Your identity has a lot to do with where you go, the people you interact with, the relationships you have, as well as the things you take ownership of in life. The process of renewing your mind, otherwise known as changing the way you think and adopting a new ideology, belief and value system, will further reinforces the image of who you desire to become and as you continue --- the new image that you desire will eventually emerge, as a result you will personify the image that has been built inside of you. This type of re-imaging does not happen over-night and requires not only your imagination but your verbal confession of who you see yourself as, coupled with meditating and musing over the new person that you desire to become.

Generally speaking people are visual and require the aid of a tangible image in front of them, this is why, as I mentioned earlier, it would serve of great benefit for you to create a vision board that will display how you see yourself dressing, the type of automobile you will drive, the house you see yourself living in, the occupation or activity you see yourself engaged in and the places you see yourself traveling too.

It is exciting to see yourself become the person you desire to be and an even greater experience as you begin to fulfill the specific unique purpose that you were born to do as you live your signature life!

As you continue forward, in your pursuit of purpose you will discover that to fully walk in the unique purpose you were born for, will require you to constantly renew your mind to who you really are and not who you were last year or ten years ago or what mistakes or shortcomings you experienced in your past. Operating in your specific unique purpose absolutely requires you to be an authentic and an original you. Do not attempt to mimic or be someone else because this will jeopardize your unique purpose, distort your desired image and diminish your true identity. Be happy and totally satisfied with who God created you to be and serve in the purpose that He designed you to do. Your unique purpose will distinguish you and cause you to shine bright.

> *"Your unique purpose will distinguish you and cause you to shine bright."*

# CHAPTER 6

∞

## 7 PREDOMINANT CATEGORIES OF PURPOSE

*Your purpose is captured in your giftings.*

*".....We are many parts of one body, and we all belong to each other.*

*In his grace, God has given us different gifts for doing certain things well. So if God has given you the ability to prophesy, speak out with as much faith as God has given you. If your gift is serving others, serve them well. If you are a teacher, teach well. If your gift is to encourage others, be encouraging. If it is giving, give generously. If God has given you leadership ability, take the responsibility seriously. And if you have a gift for showing kindness to others, do it gladly." – Romans 12:5-8 NLT*

## BORN WITH A CALL TO FUNCTION

There are a myriad of unique purposes under the sun, however, there are seven general predominant categories of purpose that are prevalent in our society today. Each one of these purposes finds their place in the systematic framework of our societal foundations---endeared as, the pillars of society or spheres of world influence.

These pillars are the influential bedrock and societal infrastructure of all nations in the world. They function as the conduit from which any nation's ideologies, core values and belief's flow through, basically, they set the tone for the way of life for a nation or country.

The lists of pillars are as follow, government, family, education, business, religion, media and arts & entertainment. Those at the helm, being the top decision makers of any one of the respective pillars, pretty much dictate the culture and expression of that pillar. Their unique purpose is woven seamlessly into the fabric of whatever respective pillar that they find their function. It is almost as though they were made to fit perfectly inside the cookie-cutter mold of the purposes they serve. Through-out my time empowering others, speaking, consulting, attending meetings and conferences, writing and studying concerning the topic of purpose I have come to discover that everyone born in the world has a unique purpose and each one of us serve in some capacity in one or more of these seven general predominant categories of purpose and were created expressly to function in one or more of the seven pillars of society.

As I share the list of the seven predominant categories of purpose keep in mind that there is no hierarchy of ranking from least to greatest, I am just listing them one after another --- they are in no order of significance.

## PURPOSED TO LEAD

The first predominant category of purpose we will discuss is the purpose to **lead**, which I also call rule. The purpose of rule is to set in order chaos, to serve as a representative, to head up a task or project, to be a founder or establish a foundation for, to pioneer and spearhead a specific cause or operation --- to be an influence, to navigate and to execute priorities. Ruler was originally taken from the Latin, to mean *straight stick* --- the guide in which all others measure and govern their activities by.

The purpose of the leader is to not only guide others but they are responsible for reproducing other leaders that are equal or greater than them. The leader is the one who sets the standard and governs over those tasks they have undertaken and are responsible for owning. The ultimate example of a leader and perfect leadership is Jesus Christ, the Son of God --- it was His selfless acts of service and love that has drawn, inspired and saved many that believed, throughout the ages. It was His works of leadership and willingness to follow the plan God had for the salvation of the world, which led the way back to us having a personal relationship with God the Father.

If we study His life and work, we quickly see that the effectiveness of His leadership was a direct result of His obedience and submission to the authority of God the Father. As a leader it is important to know the extent of your rule and understand the dynamics of authority and the role it plays in the success of any organization's corporate leadership.

One of the primary purposes of leadership is to produce other leaders. Other subsequent purposes of leadership are to govern, guide and move nations, businesses and organizations, establish trends, inspire the hopeless and set the standards of the culture.

*"The ultimate example of a leader and perfect leadership is Jesus Christ, the Son of God."*

Those whose purpose is to lead or rule have unique abilities to cause others to follow them and have a strong influence in the areas they work, deal and operate. It is not enough however to simply have influence or to exert your ability to lead in any situation but you must discover your place of leadership.

Some may start businesses and some may exercise a leadership position within a business or organization. There is a unique purpose and need for good leadership in education, business, government, arts and entertainment, politics, economics, religion, media and in every family. Some may have a specific unique purpose to become a world leader, king, ruler or president of a nation, founder, owner, or a CEO of a business or organization. Whatever the unique purpose is, as a leader or ruler you must act and serve diligently and with integrity.

Take a moment to reflect on what you just read concerning the predominant purpose to lead and rule --- if you believe this is absolutely your purpose or in any way a part of your purpose. Write down in detail why you believe that your purpose is in some way to lead or to rule in a specific capacity.

## PURPOSED TO COMMUNICATE

The second predominant category of purpose we will discuss is a **communicator**, speaker or spokesperson. Speaking is a gift that not everyone has the ability to perform well. Speaker's many times use their unique ability to communicate on the behalf of a specific person, cause or a personal conviction. Before I continue let me say that your unique purpose may be to communicate via many different communication mediums.

This ability you possess is raw and unrefined at first but if you take time to develop this gift, it will take you far. If you believe that communicating or any of the other seven predominant categories of purpose are your predominant purpose, then it is your responsibility to hone the gift you have and cultivate it to be used for the specific purpose you were intended to use it.

Also, it is important to understand that these unique abilities that are used for specific unique purposes do tend to overlap and interchange one with another.

An example of this overlapping and interchanging is that as a leader many times one may be called upon to speak or as a speaker one may be called to act in a leadership capacity to spearhead an endeavor or specific cause. The same is true for all of the seven predominant categories of purpose.

The unique purpose of communicating is fulfilled by motivationalist, activist, journalist, pastors and various other religious leaders, protestors, humanitarians and other varieties of advocacy groups as well as prophets that speak on the behalf of God to individuals, assorted people groups and to the nations of the world.

The very word communication is derived from the Latin origin, meaning *to share*. Communication is simply the activity of conveying information by the exchange of thoughts, ideas, concepts and messages through speaking, visuals, written, or behavioral mediums. It is the purposeful exchange of information shared between two or more.

The purposes of communicator's are tremendously expansive and have been instrumental in various communication technologies as well as many other profound social advancements that society currently enjoys today. These advancements in communication as we know it were key in the development of all the great civilizations and societies of the past and even up to our present-day global communication networks:

Since around 2900 BC, those with the purpose to communicate in some capacity began to develop ways in which they could document and reach further into future generations to share the thoughts and ideas of their day, so that we as the future recipients may build upon those ideas, concepts and paradigms of the past.

The most prolific of these ancient developments was paper and hieroglyphics, which enabled communicators to tell their stories and pass on information to other civilizations. Those two communication innovations would go down in history as having transformed Egyptian life and each subsequent civilization following.

Ancient Greeks loved orations, that is, the spoken word in concert. They were very good at public speaking, drama and philosophy. A lot of our western arts, turned entertainment, were inspired by the creativity and creative expression of ancient Greece.

Even until now most of the world continues to use the Roman alphabet.

In 1445, the printing press, invented by Johannes Gutenberg, aided in the rapid spread of knowledge and had a huge impact on cultural thinking across Europe and now the entire world.

Radio, film and television have had a huge influence on society in the last hundred years. And now that we have entered the age of the internet, in many ways, it has made the world smaller and a united global community.

Let us look at the predominant purpose to communicate in the lives of others in history --- their thoughts and its impact on the world.

We'll begin with Aristotle, he was quoted as saying, "*Character may almost be called the most effective means of persuasion.*"

This means that communication is not always expressed in words but the actions and deeds of an individual.

Aristotle was known for initiating the earliest model of mass communication, known as "Aristotle's Model of Communication". His introduction of this model was around 300 B.C. and it highlighted the significance of the audiences' role in communicating. This model was more focused on public speaking than interpersonal communication but the principle of relaying information from one person to another still applies.

How about Martin Luther, he was quoted as saying. *"You are not only responsible for what you say, but also for what you do not say."* His ability to communicate through his writings and public speaking was critical during the Protestant Reformation and lead to the reform and conversion of the many Catholic's to the Protestant Way, as we know it.

Sir Winston Churchill said, *"We are masters of the unsaid words, but slaves of those we let slip out."* And Dr. Martin

Luther King, Jr., through his many speeches, advocated for civil rights for all people. During one of his speeches he said, "*In the end, we will remember not the words of our enemies, but the silence of our friends.*" As a communicator it is imperative that you communicate via whatever medium --- truthfully, accurately and timely.

Take a moment now to reflect on what you just read concerning the predominant purpose to communicate and if you believe this is absolutely your purpose or in any way a part of your purpose. Write down in detail why you believe that your purpose is in some way to communicate or speak in a specific capacity.

## PURPOSED TO SERVE AND SUPPORT

The third predominant category of purpose we will look at is to **serve**, support or acts of ministerial work. This category is vast and is a category that encompasses many unsung heroes and heroine. These are people who we come in contact with each and every day of our lives. They are people we count on in clutch situations, whose presence in our lives mean a lot and without these people things just do not get done.

These are also, in a more expansive function of this purpose, the many entrepreneurs that provide goods and services throughout the world. If we had to identify those whose role is exemplified in this category of support, they would be represented by mother's, father's, sister's, brother's, aunts, uncles, cousins, friend's, co-worker's, even strangers who we may never see again. Their purposes are extremely relevant however, these specific and unique purposes may never make the evening news or headline any newspaper or magazine, these are the people that never see the glitz, glam and fame of life and their names may never by recorded in the history books of the world, yet these are the ones who if not for their existence the course of history would be forever altered and completely changed.

There was a movie made many years ago of a gentleman that fell on hard times in his life as a result of misplaced funds from his bank, at the advent of this unfortunate mishap in his life and business, he wished that he were never born. As he pondered this unfathomable thought, his wish to have never been born was granted and he was afforded the opportunity to experience what life would have been like in this world without his existence.

To his surprise he discovered that because of his absence in the world, the lives of his kin and those he knew where altered drastically even to the point of ruin and demise.

On one occasion he saved his brothers' life from a terrible accident, several years later his brother went on to perform a daring act of heroism that saved an entire naval ship and its crew from certain death during World War II ---had he not been there his brother likely would have died as a result of that terrible accident and years later, that navy vessel would not have escaped death, and would have been destroyed and thousands of lives with it. He had many friends and family that had he not been in existence, would have suffered greatly because of his absence.

In fact, as a result of his life and the significant purpose he served more than half of the entire land that his town was built on was not made to be a cemetery but rather, it was used for the development of a housing community.

He had such a significant and impactful role in the lives of others and in his community that life in that small town would not have been the same without him.

So you see, just like the man in the story I told, you really do matter, you are tremendously significant and an important contributor to the collective process and forward progress of the world as we know it. There are countless stories and accounts just like the one written above. Your purpose may not be to speak before the masses or lead a sports team to victory or travel to the moon but through your purpose to serve, support and perform ministerial works your purpose may be to write the speech for the speaker who speaks before the masses or clean the stadium where the victory of the sports team was won or to serve in some capacity at the lift off sight where a space shuttle is launched. You are important and you absolutely matter!

Let's look deeper at these words serve and service, they were originally from the Latin meaning *slave*. The selfless act of helping or performing a work for someone as in a system of supplying a public or personal need --- that is the essence of serving. When discussing the topic of service as a purpose there are many people that come to mind, however, for this example I would like to look at Ray Kroc.

Before Ray Kroc began the business of building a hamburger empire he was a kitchen equipment salesman. In 1954, at the age of 52, he came in contact with a small family owned and operated restaurant just outside of Los Angeles, California. That small family owned and operated business was McDonald's restaurant. Once Mr. Kroc bought out the McDonald brothers, he began to utilize their concept of a limited-menu, fast service and low prices and spread it out across the United States. While in the process of creating and developing the fast-food industry, he served as a model of service and excellence, second to none. Ray Kroc was quoted as saying, *"The definition of salesmanship is the gentle art of letting the customer have it your way."*

While on the topic of service as a purpose and its relationship to business, King Croesus, ancient ruler of Asia Minor, a kingdom of Lydia in the 6$^{th}$ century B.C., is credited with minting the world's first coinage. This was an advancement in the progress of how the system of business in performed today--- with the exchanging of goods and services for currency. Business and commerce would never be the same as a result of his insertion of minted currency into the market.

So you see, what you do today in fulfilling your unique purpose will be left to future generations as a legacy of your name and work. No matter how large or small the assignments we are tasked with in life, it is important to never lose sight of your worth and significant value. One word from your mouth may be all another person needs to make it another day or your winning smile could be the thing to brighten a co-workers day. One great idea from you could be so innovative and cutting-edge that the lives of all those in the world would totally be revolutionized.

So make it a point to earnestly discover your purpose, we are waiting on you.

As a supporter you may play-out your unique purpose within any of the other seven categories of purpose ---perhaps within a business, institution, organization or personally with your own family or amongst your network of associates, colleagues and friends. Here are some other ways we see purposes of service, support and ministerial works played-out --- through administrators, secretaries, general construction laborers, publishers, actors, entertainers, athletes, assistants and employee staff and faculty at all levels.

Now take a moment to reflect on what you just read concerning the predominant purpose of support and ministerial works. Do you believe this is absolutely your purpose or in any way a part of your purpose. Write down in detail why you believe that your purpose is in some way to serve or support in a specific capacity.

## PURPOSED WITH THE GIFT TO TEACH

The fourth predominant category of purpose is **teaching**. This is a category of people that are compelled to impart knowledge, share skill secrets and techniques, cultivate minds by placing a demand on the student by extracting the essence and substance of a person out of them for them to be exhibited for their own benefit and by extension the benefit of others. Those with the purpose to teach also are used to open mentally and spiritually blind eyes, cause people to understand ---and unveil truth. Teachers also have an insatiable thirst for knowledge and a genuine desire for learning and increasing their intrinsic potential.

Teachers appear in society in various forms and fashions. They serve an incomparable purpose that is paramount for the advancement of society. Without teachers the privilege of growing would be stagnated and our development would cease.

The original meaning of teaching was, *to show* ---To provide instruction by precept, example or experience --- there were many great men and women who served the purpose of teaching but this person who I will highlight next took a generation of

111

former slaves and turned many of them into millionaires. He not only taught but demonstrated how to become of indispensible value to the world around you. This person is non-other than Booker T. Washington. Raised up as a leader during the times that most African-Americans did not know how to read or write, Booker T. Washington's prolific achievements in education extended far beyond the classroom ---he also taught the value of hard work and the glory in labor.

He taught that one should not only be skilled in intellectual studies but also in a skilled-trade as a craftsman of some sort. He is quoted as saying, *"I soon learned that there was a great difference between studying about things and studying the things themselves, between book instruction and the illumination of practical experience."* It was this mindset and attitude that began Tuskegee Institute, that later became Tuskegee University. Booker T. Washington began his work and purpose to build this prestigious University with seemingly nothing. He took an old run-down church in a forest of many acres in 1881 and by 1915, he had built by hand, well over 100 buildings, had an enrollment of 1,500 students, a faculty of 200 that administrated and taught 38 trades and professions with a school financial endowment of close to $2 million dollars. His purpose and ultimate fulfillment of destiny has left a legacy that many have become heir too.

Understand that in talking about the purpose of teaching we are not only referring to classroom teachers but those who cause us to think outside of ourselves and ignite a passion in us to grow and do more. There are mentors that teach us many times during informal settings. We then become their protégé. These mentors serve as teachers and instructors in the classroom of life. Through their experiences and journeys we grasp greater insight and depth of whatever we seek to gain from them. There imparted knowledge accelerates our time and allows us to move ahead more rapidly by building on the foundation that they laid, it paves the road that we travel.

Educators have a specific unique purpose in giving us the tools and information required to frame and build our future. Instructors serve a purpose of allowing us to shadow them as an apprentice and thereby picking up the necessary skills to go on our own and be an instructor for someone else. Professors herald knowledge of their specific course discipline and subject matter mastery to students desiring to endeavor to venture into related industry niche segments. Research writers teach us through their pen with journals and books for us all to learn and discover more expansively our topic of choice.

Reflect for a moment on what you just read concerning the predominant purpose of teaching and if you believe this is absolutely your purpose or in any way a part of your purpose. Write down in detail why you believe that your purpose is in some way to teach in a specific capacity.

## PURPOSED WITH THE GIFT TO ENCOURAGE AND BUILD

The fifth predominant category of purpose is to encourage or to **build**. Builders are people of great vision and passion. You may find that a lot of people with the specific unique purpose to encourage and build always have something nice to say about people and look at their situations and circumstances with great hope and faith. The builders' purpose in many instances is to lay foundation, erect, fortify, empower, refine, train, coach, equip, furnish, supply, provide, deliver, establish and organize.

The word encourager is derived from the French as a combination of two words meaning *to place courage inside* another ---to provide strength, confidence and hope to and for someone. Building is a function that every encourager performs, it is what encourager's do ---they input courage and many times erect positive and healthy esteem in the lives of all they touch. One meaning of the word build is taken from a Greek word '*oikodomeo*', meaning to build, build up, rebuild, a physical edifice ---by extension, to edify, strengthen another person's life through acts and words of love and encouragement

115

and to embolden. I also discovered a Hebrew word for build, it is '*bana*', it simply means, to make, build, rebuild, establish, repaired, set up, surely built, to have children and to obtain children. By understanding what the words' original use is, we clearly see how it applies to an encourager.

The purpose of encouragers can be seen throughout the world and serves as an evident force of change and significant societal impact. We see this played out in the life of Albert Lutuli, a South African teacher and politician who served as the President of the African National Council (ANC) --- he built hope into the oppressed and marginalized Blacks in South Africa by leading the opposition to the White minority government, in their struggle against apartheid in South Africa. In 1960, he was awarded the Nobel Peace prize for his non-violent aggression against apartheid. Albert Lutuli was the first African to win the Nobel Peace prize.

Mother Teresa was another builder of societal comfort --- she was a missionary to the nation of India. Her undying work to build up the hurting, suffering and abandoned of the world had major impact on the youth of the world, by 1996, Mother

Teresa's impact was felt in more than 100 countries as she operated more that 500 mission orphanages throughout the world. By the end of Mother Teresa's life she was operating roughly 450 mission centers all over the world. She named her organization "Missionaries of Charity", which exemplified her mission and purpose to serve as an encourager and builder by building up the poorest of the poor in the world.

Her purpose and mission was first felt in the United States of America when she opened a mission center in the South Bronx, in New York City and by 1984 she had 19 centers all across the US.

These same words used to describe builders of humanity are mirrored as we take a look at builders of natural physical structures. These builders are people who have a creative and pioneering spirit ---their structural expressions are seen literally all around the world. These structures and more importantly there designers and builders date back to over five-thousand years ago, even all the way up to our present day. Some of the most prominent structures, edifices' and designs in the world such as the megalithic passage tomb at Newgrange in Ireland,

Stonehenge and Westminster Abbey in England, the great Sphinx and Pyramids of Egypt, the Parthenon in Greece, the Colosseum and Pantheon in Rome, Alhambra in Spain, Notre-dame de Paris and the Eiffel Tower in France, Taj Mahal in India, The Great Wall of China in China, the Empire State building and the Chrysler building in New York city, the Willis Tower (Sears Tower) and Smurfit-Stone building in Chicago and Mount Rushmore in South Dakota ---these structures represent the creativity, innovation, daring ambition and vision of builders all around the world.

We see their purpose evident as they remain throughout time as a legacy of their God-given purpose to design and build. We should celebrate the gifting of the architect, carpenter, plumber, electrician, welders and metal workers, cement, concrete, stone and brick masons, surveyors, glazier, painter, flooring specialist and interior designers. They all comprise those whose predominant purpose is to be a builder of physical structures.

Builders and encourager's often times possess a very optimistic outlook and have the unique ability to see beyond their current circumstances. Builders put feet on ideas that cause the world to move forward, they help us take our dreams and blue prints of life from concept to actuality, making dreams come true and realities exist.

We see the purposes of builders in action through founders of organizations, as they see a need and immediately begin to address the need head on ---performing the ground work necessary to see progress.

Community organizers are the ones who through grass-root efforts initiate a movement to accommodate the needs of the people in particular neighborhoods and communities.

In a more literal sense contractors and tradesman build our residential, commercial and industrial areas of living and working. Builders serve a key role in the development and growth of any organization, community, city and nation.

As an encourager one may be used in the development and building of the esteem and self-image of others. Encouragers take truths and foundational principles, using them to transform entire nations through training and demonstrating the use and correct application of them.

Builders work very effectively from the inside out. Working from the inside out means that builders are not surface people but rather, people of depth and they have the ability to see potential, draw it out, develop it and refine it to be of significant use. They take raw materials, assemble them and create value thereby.

Another example of the purpose of an encourager and builder is a personal physical fitness trainer. These individuals are in most cases highly motivated and passionate about what they do. They take on the task of sculpting bodies and boosting esteems all at the same time, they seek to discover the underlying issues of their clients eating and fitness shortcomings and errors, then set goals, cause the client to press past themselves and accomplish their goals. They teach their clients to value themselves, while establishing a sense of worth and dignity within them.

It is not uncommon to see those who serve in the purpose of building, also gifted with the unique ability to lead.

## THE BEAUTY OF LIVING ON PURPOSE ---YOUR SIGNATURE EXPRESSION

Understanding your purpose leads to a fulfilled life and causes you to plan your paths more consciously and walk with great intentionality as you seek opportunities to serve in your unique ability. I would like to again take this time to reiterate that no one should box themselves into one or two of these seven predominant categories of purpose. These are general categories and do not represent any one specific unique purpose but rather identifies and highlights various unique abilities that demonstrate how an individuals' unique purposes are played out in society.

It could be that each one of these categories may be played out in some capacity by one individual in their lifetime and at various stages throughout their development, however, as stated before it is up to you to pay attention to which one is your specific area of strength and seems to continue to emerge as most dominant in your life.

Reflect on what you just read concerning the predominant purpose of encouraging and building and if you believe this is absolutely your purpose or in any way a part of your purpose. Write down in detail why you believe that your purpose is in some way to encourage or to build in a specific capacity.

## PURPOSED TO INNOVATE

The sixth predominant category of purpose is to innovate or create, I like to simply say **giving**. When someone creates or invents something it is not simply for them but for the greater of society. For the most part these creations and inventions contribute to the convenience, comfort, accessibility or solutions for us as a global society in some way. Not only does it cause our lives to become easier but it advances our thinking and creates a ripple effect through re-engineering. These are the people whose purpose is to revolutionize the way we live and how we see our future. So for that reason I have named this category of purpose giving.

Traditionally when we think of those who are givers in a narrow sense of the word ---we have viewed them as philanthropist, however, I would like to invite you to open your mind to the idea that those who create and innovate are just as much givers as the philanthropist. By definition a philanthropist is one whose efforts are toward the advancement of human well-being through charitable gifts and endowments. The philanthropist purpose is benevolence towards man-kind.

Philanthropy is one specific unique purpose of giving. As we broaden our scope of the category of giving lets continue to identify other purposes that flow from this category of purpose, I call giving. A musician gives us music, which provide inspiration, motivation, sets a specific tone and atmosphere and can even provide an atmosphere of learning. An artist gives us their impression of the world through creating in whatever arena they may be involved. Scientists and researchers give us results of their findings as they seek to gather answers to life questions through deduction and all other empirical data.

Let's unfold the word innovator, from the Latin, *Novus* or *Novare* meaning "*new or to make new*". These inventive minds create and present the "new" to society. They have a purpose in contributing to the forward progression in modernizing society. They have a gift to think beyond the bounds of impossibility and create limitless feats. They view problems as opportunities and seldom if ever, take no, for an answer.

One of these boundless thinkers was a key player in the history and formation of America. I am referring to Benjamin Franklin, who was credited with inventing the lightning rod and bifocals.

Two other iconic inventive minds were Steve Jobs and Steve Wozniak who introduced their multi-billion dollar invention to the world from the confines of a garage. Their inventive minds led them to their ultimate purpose in commercializing computer technology throughout the world. How could anyone ever over-look the invention of the internet, credited to Vint Cerf and Bob Kahn ---their invention has caused the world to become a large connected community both socially and in business.

The list would be nearly in-exhaustive if I were to name all of the great inventors of the past and present, the likes of Galileo, Johannes Gutenberg, Eli Whitney, the Wright brothers, Elijah McCoy, Madame CJ Walker, Bill Gates, Paul Allen, these and multitudes of others all had purposes to create the conveniences, comforts and solutions that we enjoy today.

Albert Einstein, an iconic inventor himself, once said, *"only a life lived for others is a life worthwhile"*, it is that statement that personifies the sharing and value-based giving that this purpose in many ways represents.

Your purpose of giving could also likely be expressed through the giving of your time, efforts, finances, ideas or, you name it.

As a giver your entire motive is to give and contribute with the utmost generosity. Givers never run out and will never go broke because as much as they give, it seems to always be replenished.

Givers share themselves and all they have with others; they recognize that what God has given them is not to be hoarded by them but to be shared with others.

> *"Givers share themselves and all they have with others..."*

Reflect on what you just read concerning the predominant purpose of innovating and creating or what I call giving and if you believe this is absolutely your purpose or in any way a part of your purpose. Write down in detail why you believe that your purpose is in some way to be a giver in a specific capacity.

## PURPOSED TO ADVOCATE

The seventh predominant category of purpose is to advocate or what I call **mercy**. Those motivated by mercy in many cases have an interest in the justice of others. They need no reason to advocate for another except for the fact that they see an injustice being done. Those whose purpose is mercy serve as advocates for those who cannot seem to defend or represent themselves. Some purposes identified of those who are lead by mercy may include activists for various causes and social movements. Attorneys, who advocate in the courtroom on behalf of their clients, physicians who advocate in the hospitals and labs for patients, against diseases and illnesses and the list goes on, generally speaking, of those who advocate on any level.

To further give details concerning what it means to advocate, let's discover its origin. Advocate is from the Latin, meaning *to summon for counsel* or *to call to defend* on behalf of another unable to defend themselves. An exemplary illustration of those who serve in this purpose and act of mercy is the parable of the Good Samaritan. The Good Samaritan showed compassion for the helpless individual lying on the side of the road. He took ownership of the fact that he was his brother's keeper and was in some capacity responsible for the wellbeing of his neighbor.

Other examples of this purpose performed in the world today are people like Frances Wisebart Jacobs, Rev. Myron W. Reed, William J.O'Ryan, Dean H. Martyn Hart and Rabbi William S. Friedman ---these gap-standers came together in 1887 to advocate for the less-fortunate in the city of Denver, Colorado and formed an organization known today as the United Way.

Another prominent example of the impact of this purpose is the American Red Cross, founded in the United States in 1881 by a lady named Clara Barton in Washington, DC. These two examples are not even a fraction of the number of advocacy agencies in the world that are standing in the gap for under-served, marginalized, disabled, segments of society who are unable to defend themselves or protect their own rights. The purpose of the advocate does not stop at agencies and organizations but also the countless acts of kindness, compassion and mercy shown all over the world by men and women who advocate for and on the behalf of others daily.

As I mentioned earlier in this section, the parable of the Good Samaritan ---in this story, it is told of a man who was stripped, robbed and beaten up. One man saw the injured and near dead man lying in the street and crossed over to the other side of the street avoiding him. Another man walked along the same way and saw the half-conscious man bleeding in the street then he too crossed to the other side of the street to avoid him. A third man came traveling along that same road and saw the bleeding, non-responsive man ---pitied him and had mercy on him.

He went out of his way to get to him, bandaged his wounds, transported the man to a place where he would receive some medical attention and left money with the attendant for the charges that the wounded man incurred, he also mentioned that because this man was an indigent he would cover all other expenses that may be added to the man's charge.

In this story the man who went out of his way had a specific unique purpose to see to it that the man who was helpless and hopeless and yes, a stranger, received help, in an effort to see that hope was restored to him.

There are many other points to be made in this story, however, the point I would like to reflect on here is the fact that mercy lead this man to help the helpless and serve as an advocate to him.

Now take a moment to reflect on what you just read concerning the predominant purpose of mercy and if you believe this is absolutely your purpose or in any way a part of your purpose. Write down in detail why you believe that your purpose is in some way mercy in a specific capacity.

## JOURNEY TO SIGNATURE LIVING

To sum up the point of purpose and your discovery of it, ultimately leading you toward reaching your destiny, there are a few steps that are paramount in the achievement of discovering your purpose.

This first step is a matter of your own personal belief, as was key in my own personal journey --- the others are simply indicators leading to your general purpose which will eventually enlighten you to your specific unique purpose. The first is keep in mind to first ask God to show you why you were born and what impact you were designed to have in this world and with what people you will be used to impact.

The second is to reflect back on your life and identify the theme of your life, that is, what common set of occurrences seem to often surface in your life ---the types of people you attract, the types of problems you seem to always have the ability to solve, the types of activities you are drawn to and that are drawn to you and the environments you find yourself comfortable in.

Additionally, what do you do well and effortlessly and that also brings you great joy and fulfillment.

*"...First ask God to show you why you were born..."*

It may be that your purpose is something that you may not be good at now but the idea of you doing that "thing", whatever it is, brings a feeling of joy and happiness to you.

The third and equally important as the second is not to despise or ignore the predominant and re-emerging theme of your life.

# CHAPTER 7

∞

## Vision: The Eye of Your Purpose

*But seek ye first the kingdom of God, and his righteousness; and all these things shall be added unto you.-Matthew 6:33 KJV*

**We cannot talk about Destiny without first discovering Purpose ---and Purpose is conceived by Vision!**

As God's creation, we must understand, based on my definition of purpose --- *the original intent by design of a creator or manufacturer of any person, place or thing* ---that it is God who has designed us for a specific use and intent. We were in the mind of God before time ever began and he had a plan for the life that He gave us. He has a mapped out path already prepared for us that includes all the days of our lives on the earth and in

135

order for us to come in alignment with this path we must adopt the vision He has for us---thereby we achieve real success. Success means to complete your assigned tasks and fulfill your God ordained destiny. I define destiny as ---the relationships, places and stages one transition's to through-out the course of their life as a result of them fulfilling their unique purpose.

So view purpose as the *goal*....and destiny as the *prize or the end of your purpose*!

Imagine a football field, on each end of the field there is a goal-line, when a team crosses that goal-line, we call it a touchdown because they entered the end-zone.

*"View purpose as the goal and destiny as the prize."*

The end-zone in this case can be looked at as a milestone or a successful achievement on your destiny journey. Each time you score a touchdown it can be correlated to you closing a deal, getting a big break, establishing a strategic relationship that will further assist you in meeting your goals, completing a major project or simply helping someone else meet their goal.

The more touchdowns you score the more accomplished you become and the more closer you come to successfully completing your course in life.

The Apostle Paul said it this way, "I have fought a good fight, I have finished my course, I have kept the faith: (2 Timothy 4:7 KJV). What course was the Apostle Paul speaking of? He was referring to his destiny and the fulfillment of his purpose, God told him that his purpose was to bear his name before the Gentiles, and kings and the children of Israel. Acts 9:15 reads, concerning the Apostle Paul, *"But the Lord said unto him, Go thy way: for he is a chosen vessel unto me, to bear my name before the Gentiles, and kings, and the children of Israel..."*

## YOUR VISION OF PURPOSE AND DESTINY

The way you see yourself is the way that you will live your life. The way that you view your gifts and abilities will dictate how you utilize them. If you celebrate the giftings that God has given you and work to master them then they will work for you and bring you before great men. If you do not celebrate your giftings and abilities and never work to improve and master them then you will live an unfulfilled and frustrated life. To live on purpose it is imperative that you release your potential and master your life. The essence of mastery is to understand and be able to articulate with greater distinction than another on any given subject matter or topic. To gain mastery over your life you must be able to distinctly identify and understand the unique giftings and abilities that you possess and your ability to definitively articulate that --- not just in words but in the expression of your life. This is where vision comes into play and its connection to you reaching your destiny and fulfilling your purpose to live your signature life.

## THE VISIONARY STEWARD

Based on the parable of the talents as told in the Holy Bible, we can gather clues on the impact that vision has on an individual fulfilling their purpose and reaching their destiny. Lets peer into this story told over two-thousand years ago by Jesus, as He was teaching his disciples the importance of stewardship, ownership and effectively utilizing the gifts, talents and abilities that they

138

have been given to produce profit. God has invested within each one of us the gifts and tools that are necessary for us to build on His foundation, in His Kingdom.

The story begins with the master entrusting talents (gifts) to three servants, meaning those who owned nothing. To one servant He gave five talents, to the second servant He gave two talents and to the third servant He gave one talent. All the servants were given gifts, merited according to their several ability, more specifically, their unique capacity to handle the gifting given to them. While the master was gone on a trip for a long time, the person with five talents doubled his and made ten talents; the person with two talents doubled his and made four talents; the person with one talent hid (buried) his, made nothing and the one *talent* he had was given to the one who had the most talents.

In this story, talents represent gifts, these gifts were to be used for a specific purpose. As I stated earlier in the book, your purpose is always captured in your giftings, so purpose could be represented by the talents as well. Destiny is represented by the servants doubling their talents and entering into a level of mastery by achieving their objective, to profit from the original investment. Vision in this illustration is the picture of a foreseen reality ---the reality of actualizing their dream.

In this parable, told by Jesus, the two servants who attained mastery by reaching their destiny, saw something... let me ask you...what did they see? It is obvious ---they saw themselves doubling their talents. What do you see in your life?

Life truly is what you make it ---but the question is how do you view your life and where does this picture or your view of it, take you?

*"What do you see in your life?"*

When you change the way you see things, the things you see change...... You must see your life as more than just a series of unrelated events! ---Life must become purposeful to you.

You have to have a vision in order to go anywhere in life! Let me further define vision ---Vision is a mental picture, vision is a function of your heart utilizing your imagination, vision is a source of hope. Once you have received true vision and it becomes clear to you, it takes over your life! Your vision fosters self-discipline, this discipline protects the vision that you have adopted as your own. Vision build image, it creates and reinforces character in the life of the visionary.

*"Life must become purposeful to you!"*

Over and above all other decisions you make, your vision centers you and causes you to make decisions in line with getting you to where you need to be.

Clear vision helps you to keep the good ideas that come up from time to time, from becoming distractions to your unique purpose that has you on course to reaching your destiny!

To manifest vision you must act as if it has already taken place.

You have to see yourself as that ---teacher, lawyer, engineer, millionaire, billionaire, mother, father, actor, actress and so on and so forth.

141

## VISION IS ESSENTIAL TO YOUR SUCCESS

Vision is given to us as a directional guide, it is used as our internal GPS system and it sees only possibilities. It never acknowledges impossibilities because in the realm of vision there are no impossibilities. It looks through situations and envisions how it can glorify God!

When we shine and rise to the top of our game, people notice that, and it serves as a reflection of the greatness of God in us and the gifts, talents and abilities that He has given us to work with and to help others. Vision comes with understanding and instructs us to look past the exterior of people, to discover what really makes them tick and press beyond seemingly difficult circumstances, to get to the other side.

If you are going to succeed through your course in life, you must have a clear vision and strong Faith. The picture you have in your imagination will only become the reality you live, by first believing that it is possible for you to achieve. To the visionary their vision is there reality!

You must often encourage yourself along the way, as the reality of your vision begins to manifest in your life. The vision you have, if clear and well defined, will serve as a sense of pure inspiration to you. The impact of inspiration in your life can be described as when the faith you have in your idea, dream or vision takes hold of you and moves you to take action.

Subsequent to the excitement produced from this injection of pure inspiration, you become motivated ---the impact of motivation in your life can be described as when you take hold of your idea, dream or vision and you move it into action.

The inspiration produced in your life from your vision will motivate you to take the one-dimensional image you have in your imagination and create from it a three-dimensional reality that you live each day!

Vision creates tremendous self-discipline in the life of the visionary!

Vision is always given to one on behalf of many. This can be seen through the accounts of history all over the world. The vision that God gives one is always used to impact many, as in the lives of Abraham, Joseph, Moses, Nehemiah, Apostle Paul, Jesus, Abraham Lincoln, Booker T Washington, Dr. Martin Luther King Jr., countless others and You! Yes, you have a part to play in the course of history in your world and sphere of influence. Scripture tells us in Proverbs 29:18, "Where there is no vision, the people perish..."(KJV). Let's analyze this throughout the history of the world. We will begin with Abraham of the Bible.

> *"Vision creates tremendous self-discipline in the life of the visionary!"*

Abraham – a nation was formed through him...Joseph – a nation was spared because of him...

Moses – a nation was freed from bondage and slavery because of him...

Nehemiah – a city was restored because of him...

Apostle Paul – the world was evangelized because of him...

Jesus Christ – the world was redeemed and saved because of him...

Abraham Lincoln – Slaves were freed because of him…

Booker T. Washington – former slaves became Millionaires because of him….

Dr. Martin Luther King Jr. – Blacks were afforded civil rights because of him…

You – who will you be used to free, serve, lead, protect, teach, develop, empower…..

Clear vision makes one a specialist as they will have gained mastery in whatever area they are purposed to impact their world, through diligence in their pursuit to their destiny.

As you live on purpose, guided by the vision you have adopted as your own, the idea of being in the wrong place at the wrong time is relatively diminished because the vision you possess will lead you to success and victory all of the time! ---you will be led to be in the right place at the right time in your right mind!

145

If you are living your life solely on what you see with your eyes --- your sensory perceptive organ --- you are totally missing out on the life you were ordained by God to live!

God is always speaking to us --showing us pictures of our divine future. He always speaks in pictures. You have heard the phrase, "picture yourself doing this or doing that".... Or "a picture is worth a thousand words"...

> *"God is always speaking to us."*

If I said to you that you are winning in life! What picture comes to your mind? Not everybody is going to have the same picture in mind ---what is your vision or picture of winning?

Keeping the vision in front of you will cause you to become unstoppable in your pursuit of making it a reality for you.

Get yourself a vision board and update it often.

## CREATE AND DEVELOP YOUR OWN PERSONAL VISION BOARD

Your vision board serves as the tangible picture of your future. Some have a literal board others have a physical object that serves as a constant reminder of the thing they would like to attain. For instance, as strange as it may sound, an aspiring singer may purchase a microphone to keep them in remembrance of their dream to be a successful singer, a college student may have a cap and gown hanging in their closet to keep them pressing toward the goal of graduating, still other's may have a model car or a model airplane or a model house to keep the passion strong within them of one day attaining the material object that they desire or perhaps someone else's vision may be to become an influence in a specific sphere, field or industry that they are involved.

Here are some easy steps to create your own personal vision board. First you must answer these questions ---where do you desire to go? What do you desire to do? Who do you desire to impact? When do you desire for this to happen? Why do you desire this?

Identify people who are successful at doing what it is that you desire to do, find out how they did it ---adopt the attitude that, 'if anybody can do it, I can too'!

Invest in books, audio programs, CD's and even subscribe to magazines that are related to your industry and become knowledgeable about things in your industry or the area in life that you desire to grow, as well as the person that you desire to become.

Get pictures and clippings that reflect images of where you see yourself ---for instance, if you see yourself speaking before audiences, select pictures of others speaking before audiences and envision that it is you, or if you desire to have a wardrobe of fine apparel, then select pictures of the apparel that you desire and post them to your board as a vision of how you desire your closet to look. These are just a couple of examples to get you started. Have fun and don't stop until you meet your goals!

## VISION IS ESSENTIAL TO YOU REACHING YOUR DESTINY

Vision narrows your view and causes you to become intently focused on achieving the goal before you. It reduces the risk for you of coming off track or being distracted as you move toward attaining the goal you have in your heart to accomplish.

Recklessness in a person's life is the result of them having no vision. People experience a chaotic and aimless life, which lead them to dead-ends many time because there is no consistency and focus in their lives. When you have no vision you constantly change, this changing is primarily because there is no focal point to which you are anchored. This focal point fastens you to your goal

*"When you have no vision, you constantly change."*

so that you may stay the course, remain on task and turn the picture in your imagination into your current reality and state of life.

Vision sees your future in your present ---this means that your vision has the potential to reveal to you how to meet goals by performing the objectives that are necessary to overcome the obstacles that present themselves before you on the highway of destiny. Vision is the very blueprint of your future. Vision is a clear picture of your unique purpose.

True vision is given to us by God, as our unique part to play in God's masterful plan to perfect His will in the earth.

*"True vision is given
to us by God."*

It's all about accomplishing the purpose that God has sent us into the earth to fulfill. In 2 Corinthians 10:5, the amplified version of scripture tells us to bring our thoughts and purpose into the obedience of Christ ---this means that your gifts, talents and abilities must be submitted to the will of God to be used for His original purpose for you. God has given us ownership rights as stewards over our giftings but expects us to bring them in alignment with His perfect will for our lives. He has the master plan for us. For us to be truly successful, we must follow His plan for our lives and use the gifts that He has given us, according to His master plan.

# CHAPTER 8

∞

## Your Distinctive Path to Destiny

*There is a way which seemeth right unto a man, but the end thereof are the ways of death.-Proverbs 14:12 KJV*

**GOAL SETTING** - The Path to Destiny

**If you desire to accomplish anything in life, you are going to have to move in the direction of your desired result, good intentions alone has never gotten anyone, anywhere.**

There is a saying that goes, 'you cannot hit a target that you cannot see.' In life, as your destiny unfolds, it is paramount that you develop a plan to accomplish the vision, or let's say the target, that you have for your life. How do you plan to land at success if you haven't identified how success looks for you?

Goal setting is used as a measuring tape or road marker as you journey to success. Studies have shown that 80% of people never set goals and of the 20% that remain, only 70% ever follow-through to the completion of the goals they have set for themselves. Think about it, how does one expect to win in life if they never plan or set goals? It is said that a sign of insanity is to do the same thing and expect different results. Achieving greatness in life is not accidental ---it is done with intentionality, strict discipline, a regimented lifestyle, precision focus and some really good breaks, that is a part of what it takes to get to top.

> *"...how does one expect to win in life if they never plan or set goals?"*

No one sets out on a journey without a roadmap or a compass and no one makes it to the top of a mountain without planning, preparation and strategic goal setting before ever taking their first steps. Likewise, in life to reach the top or peak of your potential, ultimately your destiny, it will take more doing than simply hoping.

## THE STARTING POINT ---"YOU ARE HERE"

Let's review a few terms for clarity. First, we must know what a goal is, a goal is a set mark or drawn target. The way to meet your goals, your set mark and drawn target is by devising feasible objectives, an objective is the means by which any goal is accomplished. Some goals are short-term and other goals are long-term. A long-term goal, relatively speaking is anywhere from 13 months and beyond ---a short-term goal is traditionally somewhere between 30 days to 12 months.

Creating objectives to meet those goals is strategic and requires thought. Many times in life we try to figure out why things happen ---sometimes we see why and other times we may not, however, as our destiny's unfold, in a weird sort of way, all the things that happened to us in our life begins to make sense in retrospect. As we reflect back we can see how one decision, event or relationship led to another and that decision, event, relationship or circumstance led to another and another, all the way to our present day.

Without understanding your unique purpose all of these
occurrences in your life may seem unrelated or coincidental but
once you understand your unique purpose, you can then connect
the dots and begin to make sense out of it all. As you begin to
assemble these seemingly random parts in your life, you can
now locate yourself, gather your bearings and chart your course
as best you can.

As you chart your course there will be times that things will not
go the way you planned and that is when you must step back
and ask God how those uneventful occurrences contribute to
your collective destiny, that is, the relationships, places and
stages that you transition to throughout the course of your life
as a result of you fulfilling and performing your unique purpose.
It is your purpose that your destiny is wrapped around and in
order to truly know your purpose you must ask God, the giver
of all purpose.

Based on the definition I gave for purpose, which is, the original
intent by design of a creator or manufacturer of any person,
place or thing ---it would be impossible to figure this out on
your own. It is God that will give you a desire and passion for

something, He will reveal to you your core strengths and abilities, or He will make plain to you as you seek Him, that you are in some way already engaged in what He has planned for you to do.

So as you locate yourself, as you would find illustrated on a map or a space plan, ask God what's next, then write it down and begin to plan and set goals that are in alignment with where God is leading you to go in your life, as you positively impact others along the way.

> *"...ask God, then write it down and begin to plan and set goals that are in alignment with where God is leading you."*

## GETTING THE M.O.S.T. OUT OF LIFE

Getting the **M. O. S. T.** out of life is what masses of people are attempting to do these days but all are not succeeding. Unfortunately many are falling short of a purposeful and fulfilling life and they often settle for what is thrown at them in life. There comes a point in a person's life that they must become fed-up and say, enough is enough ---there has to be more to life that what meets the eye. You must make a decision that you desire the M.O.S.T. out of life and that you are a winner in life and that the game will not end until I win!

M.O.S.T. is an acronym that represents how to get from one place, point A to another place, point B and so on. The letters of this clever acronym stand for  **M**- mission, **O**- objective, **S**- strategy,  **T**- tactic. Now let's elaborate on each tenet of this acronym.

The mission is any assignment or task within the scope of your purpose that will land you at a specific, desired destination.

The objective, as we discovered earlier is the means by which you will accomplish your mission.

The strategy is the calculated composition and targeted direction of the objective that will gain you advantage and favorable position as it relates to the given assignment or task through the use of the resources that you desire and deem fit to employ.

The tactic is simply the implementation of the strategy that you have developed.

## MY 5-GOAL SETTING RULES

Goal setting rule #1 - locate where you currently are and then identify where you desire to be.

Goal setting rule #2 - set goals that are aligned with advancing you toward a specific target as it relates to your divine destiny.

Goal setting rule #3 - position yourself to be successful and prosper--- do not wait on someone else too!

Goal setting rule #4 - identify strategic resources and employ them where and when needed.

Goal setting rules #5 - if you fail to plan, then you have planned to fail!

## WHY SET A GOAL?

*I press toward the mark for the prize of the high calling of God in Christ Jesus.*   **-Philippians 3:14 KJV**

In order to reach the mark for any prize in life you must set goals and press to meet those goals to win the prize and move on to greater levels in life. You should not be in the same place, stage or level in your life next year that you are currently at this year and the place, stage and level you currently are located this year, should be far in advance of where you were last year.

Life is about constant progression and to become stagnant means that you are simply marking time without any advancement. Nature itself demonstrates that life moves forward and never stands still ---meaning that everything in life grows and produces more after its kind, however, if this progress ceases, then life ends for that thing.

If you plant a seed of any kind and observe it over time you will see a progression of growth that begins from seemingly nothing, as the process of germination beneath the surface of the soil occurs, you must continue looking and then the blade will emerge, then the stem, the leaf and so on ---your life is no different, there should be notable growth in your life from year to year. If no growth is evident, you should take inventory of your life and with an honest estimate, locate where you currently are, then identify where you desire to be. Create a plan and then by goal setting cause the plan to actualize in your life.

*"Locate where you are, then identify where you desire to be."*

## 5 BENEFITS OF EFFECTIVE GOAL SETTING

1. It positions you to win as seen in the lives of professional athletes, successful business people and top achievers at all levels in all fields and walks of life.

2.  Setting goals helps you to align your life with the vision that you have before you. It puts your vision within reach by using short and long-term planning strategies that can be measured and managed.

3.  Goal setting inspires you intrinsically and motivates you as you see the external results of your completed achievements.

4.  Goal setting disciplines you and acts as a time management tutor for you --- steering you clear of time wasters and distractions.

5.  Goal setting builds self-confidence at the subconscious level --- creating an image of success in your mind which causes you to become more successful and see greater victories!

## HOW DO I MEET MY GOALS?

*I have fought a good fight,* **_I have finished my course_**, *I have kept the faith*:      **-2 Timothy 4:7 KJV**

Finishing a task is essential to being successful. If you do not finish a task, assignment or level, successfully, how do you plan to start the subsequent levels and attain success within them. This is apparent in the education system as well as in the construction industry, as we witness the principle of succession being applied, this principle states, structure proceeds growth, this is extremely evident ---in order to be promoted and pass to the next grade level you must have proven successful completion of that previous grade level and objectives. Certainly on the construction site, the excavation,

> *"Finishing a task is essential to being successful."*

footing and foundation work must be performed completely to successfully build any structure on top of it. We observe this principle exercised in our social existence, with the illustration of the journey to becoming married, there is a succession of events that lead to the altar of holy matrimony.

There is a level or a goal of introduction, a level or a goal of acquaintance, a level or a goal of friendship, a level or a goal of trustworthiness established, a level or a goal of courtship, a level or a goal of love and mutual bonding established, a level or a goal of commitment that is most often followed by a level or a goal of espousal and set engagement and finally a level or a goal of marriage.

If any of these levels or goals are not successfully met, then the structure of the marriage itself could be in jeopardy, as the requirements for the levels of its foundation were not successfully met. I must add that there is no specific length of time prescribed for each level's performance to be completed with regard to the marriage.

This is just one example of how goal setting looks in the life of someone as it relates to marriage. Now utilizing this same principle of succession, apply it to your life. This is how you meet your goals.

First define your life by clearly defined statements---what I mean, is to create your own personal vision statement.

Your vision statement is a clearly written statement of your future goal aspiration and its relation to your core purpose and values.

What is your personal mission statement? This statement is a clearly written statement that outlines your unique purpose, how you plan to fulfill your unique purpose and who is impacted by your unique purpose ---the how and who in your personal mission statement will change based on the place, stage and state you are situated in your life but your core unique purpose will always remain invariable.

As I mentioned earlier, your life should be based on a set of core values and principles. List them. This list can be simply conveyed by the beliefs that shape and impact the decisions you make, the moral and ethical ground that you stand on in life and the standards that you live and conduct your life by ---items like integrity, discipline, love, commitment, determination, honor, courage and respect to name a few.

Referring back to this list will remind you of who and what you are made of when things gets rough and challenges mount in opposition to you accomplishing your goals. It's those thoughts that determine if you will succeed or fail in your goal endeavors.

Take time to manage your thoughts, you may be surprised at the tremendous impact that they have on where and how far you go in life. What thoughts do you have about your life? What vision do you have for your life? Goal setting and equally important, goal achievement is the method in which visions become reality.

*"Take time to manage your thoughts..."*

The goals you set based on your vision should clearly identify and outline your next steps in life. First, with an honest estimate locate yourself ---that is your current stage, place and state in life. The stage of your life can be described as your progression and development in life, characterized by an individual being an adolescent, young adult, middle aged or elderly. The place you may find yourself in life could be described as an individual being single, married, divorced or widowed --- this could be a person with or without children. Lastly, the state of your life could be recognized as being stagnant, confused, upwardly mobile, content, discontented or where ever you perceive yourself to be emotionally, mentally or spiritually.

To meet your goals you are going to have to write them down! (**Habakkuk 2:2**) Begin by simply brain storming --- what do you desire to do, where do you desire to go, what ideas do you desire to actualize, what relationships do you desire to build and when do you desire to accomplish each of these tasks?

Now start to organize your ideas into clusters and categorize them. Examples of this categorizing may look like this ---a category of family, personal (health), financial, spiritual, career or business, relationships, travel destinations, idea #1, idea #2, idea #3 and so on.

For each category describe as clearly and in as much detail as possible the end result of each one and what impact it will have on your life and the lives of those around you. Now begin to map-out and strategically plan how you will achieve these goals with practical and measureable objectives.

# CHAPTER 9

∞

## Actualizing Your Signature Life

*For we are his workmanship, created in Christ Jesus unto good works, which God hath before ordained that we should walk in them.-Ephesians 2:10 KJV*

## ACTUALIZING YOUR SIGNATURE LIFE

Since the beginning of creation, mankind has been designed and instructed by God to fulfill tasks by producing from their inner-potential, living from the inside out. Just as each one of us living on earth today has a separate and distinct fingerprint, so we also, all have a distinct and unique purpose to fulfill, that calling on the inside of us. Though many of us may share similar passions and may pursue like interests, we all have our very own signature execution of those passions and interests, each with exceptional impacts on the ones we affect by it.

We are all unique originals and have been loaded up with potential that resides just below the surface of our acute conscious awareness. It is our duty and sole responsibility to mine the treasures inside ourselves, in order that we may discover the hidden potential that God has placed within us all. This hidden potential is buried in our gifts and talents and when we expose them, it leads us to our unique purpose, which starts us on our course to reaching our God ordained destiny.

*"We are all unique originals and have been loaded up with potential..."*

The passion and desire that you have ---to be more and to go further in life is the calling to greatness that God has prescribed for each one of us all to attain. There is something innately in us that desires to be all that we can be. It is up to us then, to answer the call and fulfill our purpose. The fulfillment of our unique purpose is the primary reason why we were born. We all have a definite part to play in life and more particularly in the lives of those around us.

It is important that we utilize our gifts and talents in their creative expressions as we live-out our unique purpose and leave our signature mark for the generations that follow us.

> *"Everyone on the planet has their own signature way of performing their purpose and no one can take that away."*

There is no one on earth who can do what you do, the way that you do it. There may be those who can in some way imitate you but they are not you --- everyone on the planet has their own signature way of performing their purpose and no one can take that away.

As you begin to perform your purpose, you will begin to carry yourself with extreme confidence and with an enormous zeal for living ---you will begin to attract to yourself good opportunities and you will be favored among people but along with all the good things that I just listed, there will be some that hate you for the success you attain. Unfortunately, this comes with the territory. As you live your signature life, it will be as though you were literally born to do what you do ---because you were!

Those who actually discover their unique purpose and fulfill it, are considered to be self-actualized, a term used in the discipline of psychology, this term was originally introduced by Kurt Goldstein, a neurologist and psychiatrist who was a pioneer in modern neuropsychology. His theory was that all organism's have an innate motive to release their potential and express their creativity. He termed it as one's '*master motive*' --the one driving force that motivates all creation to be all they were created and designed to be.

As theories continued to be developed concerning this idea of actualization, an American psychologist named Abraham Maslow popularized this catchy idea of self-actualization and brought it to prominence in his 1943 paper entitled '*The Theory of Human Motivation*' with his famous hierarchy of needs.

Maslow's hierarchy of needs outlined, by priority, the basic human needs that are innately built into all people, designed to motivate them through-out their lives. This hierarchy of needs culminates with the idea of an individual having maximized their potential by fully developing through each stage of the tiered developmental model he created. The developmental model builds one on another beginning with psychological needs, then safety needs, then love and the need to belong, then esteem development and ending with self-actualization, mastering the preceding stages, in which he termed deficiency needs, and living life at a highly developed and mature level.

This mean that living your signature life fully encompasses the stages we just covered as well as a full awareness of your unique purpose and execution of it competently ---without being encumbered by the attitudes and opinions of other's about you. You know who you are, what you desire, where you are going, how you will get there and the impact you will make when you arrive there.

## THE SELF-ACTUALIZED SIGNATURE LIFE

Maslow chose to study the lives of those he called exemplary people. These were people that had risen to the top of their fields and industries and ascended to prominence as a result of their signature living and unique purpose. Among the list of people he selected to study were the likes of Albert Einstein and Frederick Douglass, these individuals modeled a certain level of high-distinction as they were leading signature lives that were incomparable.

It has been recorded that Maslow studied the top one-percent of college and university students during his time researching. His studies of the top achiever's in life further distinguished his characterization of the self-actualized person.

The self-actualized person can be identified by the following attributes.

*Attribute 1.* They display an acute awareness of their reality and are not mislead into believing what or who they are not ---they know who they are and are not defined by their surroundings.

*Attribute 2.* The self-actualized person tends to view problems as opportunities to create solutions and seldom if ever complain or make up excuses.

*Attribute 3.* The self-actualized person is comfortable and secure working alone or within a group on tasks and projects without feelings of inferiority among the work group.

*Attribute 4.* They do not subject their lives to popular opinion and socially acceptable views.

*Attribute 5.* They do not base their success or judgments of how far they can go in life on the experiences of others---they do not conform to their cultural environment but tend to be cultural trend setters.

*Attribute 6.* They celebrate the strengths of others and are not bias ---they embrace and honor all cultures, races and signature styles.

*Attribute 7.* They are generally compassionate and concerned with the welfare of humanity.

*Attribute 8.* They recognize the unique personalities and character of others and do not attempt to change them to fit their mold for them.

*Attribute 9.* They are happy with who they are and all of their idiosyncrasies.

*Attribute 10.* They often have a close knit community of just a small number of close friends rather than lots of surface relationships.

***Attribute 11.*** They have a healthy sense of humor.

***Attribute 12.*** They express a great zeal and passion for life and give themselves totally to their assigned task or whatever they are currently engaged in performing.

***Attribute 13.*** They are very creative, innovative and original --- they exhibit signature lives!

***Attribute 14.*** They think big, seek to maximize their potential and create opportunities that leave an impact of the legacy of their signature mark.

As you move into signature living you will develop a knowledge, understanding, appreciation and distinctive articulation of who you are, God's unique purpose for your life and your influence, effectiveness and impact will increase as you leave your signature mark in every place you go.

## OVERCOMING OBSTACLES TO SIGNATURE LIVING

What seems to stop or hinder you as you pursue your goal to live your signature life? There are as many excuses for not meeting your goal and living your signature life as there are opportunities too. In order to meet your goals, you are going to have to press toward that end. You cannot allow anything or anyone to impede your forward progress.

> *"In order to meet your goals, you are going to have to press toward that end."*

You cannot allow yourself to become a stumbling block either --- your fears, anxieties and doubts about your ability to successfully accomplish what you were born and ultimately designed to do.

You cannot allow pessimistic people and negative situations that may occur in your life to shape who you are, you must be focused on living your signature life with intentionality and purpose each day.

I have listed some common items here that we all must overcome to live a successful, rewarding and fulfilling signature life.

## TOO CHALENGING

One of the first obstacles you must hurdle is the idea that the life task that you have been charged with fulfilling is *too challenging*. God has provided His grace to cause you to do the impossible. Things that seem as though they are insurmountable become achievable as you are led by God's Holy Spirit. The Apostle Paul wrote in the book of Philippians 4:13 (*KJV*), *I can do all things through Christ which strengthens me* ---and so can you!

As you begin to operate in your unique purpose, keep the rewarding end results in mind. Remember the goal that you are seeking to accomplish. Jesus applied this same idea of keeping the big picture in mind and in perspective during trials and challenges ---in Hebrews 12:2 (*KJV*), the scripture says, *Looking unto Jesus the author and finisher of our faith; who for*

179

*the joy that was set before him endured the cross, despising the shame, and is set down at the right hand of the throne of God.*

Challenges are real but the reality of you living your signature life must become greater than the present circumstances dictate your life to be. There is greatness in you ---greater than any challenge that is placed before you. You can do it! Live your best life and fulfill your unique purpose as you enjoy signature living.

*"There is greatness in you... "*

## YOUR SIGNIFICANCE

Another obstacle to you living your signature life is the idea of *your significance.* To combat and defeat this idea that you are not significant, remind yourself of the tremendous impact that your unique purpose will have on you and those around you. You are by no means insignificant, your life and purpose is of indispensible value, you are incomparable, and there is no material possession on this earth that can come close to your unique worth.

You must convince yourself of this ---you are God's masterpiece! This is what God the awesome creator of all things says about you, *For we are God's masterpiece. He has created us anew in Christ Jesus, so we can do the good things he planned for us long ago.* (Ephesians 2:10 NLT). This means that you were on God's mind even before you were born --- that's significant!

## FEAR

*Fear* is another obstacle that you must overcome. Fear is designed to incapacitate you, put you out of action, disable, hinder, delay, isolate, immobilize, paralyze, cripple and box you in. Fear will cause you to settle when you know you can do better, it will cause you to stop when you know that you have the capacity to go further and to do more and it will cause you to bury your gifts, talents and abilities.

In the parable of the talents, the servant who was given one talent hid his, by burying it ---when the master of the servants returned and called for the servant to give account of the talent he received, he said that he buried it because he was afraid (Matthew 25:14-29).

Let me list some other names of fear that you may be familiar with, timidity, nervousness, shyness, anxiety, unease, fretful, freight, terror, dread, worry, panic, stress and procrastination. Some people put off what they know they should be doing today and use the excuse that they are not ready yet.

I am a strong proponent of planning and preparing, however, some people have no intentions to prepare, have not even began to prepare and continue to use the excuse ---I'm not ready. My question to them is, if not now, then when...?? Many times this idea not being ready or prepared yet, is rooted in fear ---could be fear of failure and even fear of succeeding.

Yes, some people fear that if they succeed they will not be able to maintain the level of success they have attained and thereby eventually fail or fall from success.

Living your signature life will absolutely require you to be fearless, disciplined and intentional. You will never achieve your goals if you never step out and begin the work to achieve them. You must have courage and confidence in knowing that you are pleasing God by accomplishing the work He has given you to do.

I define courage as taking action in spite of fear. In the Bible, in the first chapter of the book of Joshua, God commands Joshua to be of good courage and to be very courageous ---God told him this four times in the first chapter. God knew that in order for Joshua to fulfill his purpose and reach the destiny that He had prepared for him, that he was going to have to be courageous and fearless.

*"Courage is taking action in spite of fear."*

For you to fulfill your purpose and reach your destiny, you are going to have to be courageous and fearless too! There is so much more to you than is apparent but in order for the real you to show up, you are going to have to overcome every fear that opposes you, to block you in, stop you or paralyze you. To overcome this, you must know that God loves you, He is for you, He is with you and in you to accomplish every assignment, task and purpose that He has prepared for you to perform.

You are fearless, God made you that way ---He has not given you a cowardice spirit of fear and timidity but He has given you a conquering spirit of power and of love and of a sound, safe, strong, stable, wise and disciplined mind that produces only Godly thoughts of increase to accomplish the work He has prepared for you.

## CAPITAL INVESTMENT

This next one has relevant value depending on the goal or purpose you have placed before you. I'm referring to money, the *capital investment* required for you to accomplish the goals you have to meet within the scope of your unique purpose. I would first like for you to understand that contrary to the popular saying, 'it takes money, to make money' ---rather it takes a good idea to make money. There are numerous numbers of professional athletes, entertainers and lottery winner's that have had lots of cash with no idea of how or what to do with it and it has evaporated out of their lives, as quickly as it came, it departed.

I believe that the intellectual property of an individual merits a great deal more than the fact of simply possessing cash. If you have a great idea, the idea will attract the money to fund it, but if you simply have cash alone with no idea to advance or assign the money to, you actually stand in jeopardy of losing it.

In addition to this, I do not desire for you to be naïve or in any way deceived into believing that you do not need money at all because you do. In order to do most anything in this world's system it will require money ---the exchange of any commercial goods or service for domestic currency is required.

Here are a few ways to overcome this barrier in your life ---seek to build strategic relationships, learn to articulate your vision, invest some of your time and effort into the work and vision of someone else, ask God to give you favor in and with your market and have a written plan that outlines your vision, that you may share with those who would like to invest into you.

## TIME INVESTMENT

Last on my list of obstacles that you must overcome in living your signature life is the amount of *time investment* required to meet your goals in fulfilling your unique purpose. There will be considerable time invested in actualizing your signature life. Here are some tips to live by as you live your signature life, fulfill your unique purpose and reach your destiny.

Tip One: Manage your time wisely and avoid time wasters.

Tip Two: Identify how much time investment is required to meet your goal and then create a plan to carve out that time each day.

Tip Three: Create a journal that chronicles your progress.

## WISDOM, KNOWLEDGE AND UNDERSTANDING

Life has the potential to be difficult to comprehend at times. Sort of like putting together a jig-saw puzzle. When we see the picture on the puzzle box in the store it is so beautiful and it draws us to purchase it, however, when we get it home, open the wrapper and realize that there are 500 pieces to it, the challenge begins as we must set in motion the daunting task of assembling this beautiful, intricate work of art.

So it is in our lives, we see this perfect picture of how our life will be and how smoothly and fluid our life will flow, all in synch, like a symphony orchestra ---after imagining this wonderful, beautiful, perfect life of ours, we then land back at our current reality and realize all the work, resources required and opportunities to seize, it is then that the daunting task of putting it all together begins, in order to see it manifest in our life.

It is that picturesque expansive image of our lives that motivates us each day to keep pressing ahead until we arrive at the life we have envisioned and dream about.

Seeing the big picture in life helps to put things into perspective for you and can be used to measure your success along the way. Your big picture should be the picture of you fulfilling your unique purpose. It is essential that you know your unique purpose and understand your place in life. To do that successfully it takes a degree of wisdom, knowledge and understanding.

*"Seeing the big picture in life helps to put things into perspective for you and can be used to measure your success along the way."*

For this illustration concerning you living your signature life, *knowledge* can be interpreted as "the parts" of your life ---your gifts, talents, education, skills, relationships, ideas, dreams, goals and all other tangible and intangible resources that you possess. These things represent the various moving and static parts of your life.

*Understanding* then can be viewed as the assembly of those parts and how well you organize, order, arrange and prioritize these parts of your life in a way that moves you into the direction and ultimate realization of your unique purpose and signature life.

Understanding helps you connect one part of your life to another, as well as to cause them to operate synergistically. I like to call it connecting the dots of your life, so that collectively they all make sense together.

You must see your life as more than just a series of unrelated events ---understanding takes the guess-work out of your life!

Wisdom, as it relates to living your signature life, is the result of correctly appropriating the knowledge and understanding you possess in your life. Wisdom instructs you in the best path to takes for your life and guides you into sound decision making to get you exactly to the destination you are seeking.

Wisdom positions you to prosper and causes you to be favored even in the midst of unfavorable circumstances. Wisdom preserves your life and attracts wealth to you. Wisdom puts you in the right place at the right time with the right information and the right people, in optimal situations. It provides opportunities that ordinarily may not have been granted to you, it strategically cuts off excess and waste in your life.

*"Wisdom positions you to prosper and causes you to be favored even in the midst of unfavorable circumstances."*

Wisdom gives you answers and provides you with solutions that astound your peers and superiors. Wisdom is a master key to living your signature life.

Mastery of this dynamic trichotomy of wisdom, knowledge and understanding is essential to living a successful life!

This is how signature living is played out in a person's life. God will show you a picture of his promise for you. This picture may come as an idea or a dream that you have a desire to fulfill. This picture is based on His divine plan for your life as expressed in Jeremiah 29:11, this scripture states, *"For I know the plans I have for you," declares the* LORD, *"plans to prosper you and not to harm you, plans to give you hope and a future* (**NIV**).

This picture is developed in your imagination and is primarily the result of one or more of the following three basis.

## Basis #1 - Vision of some <u>Natural Giftings</u> You Perform Well

This is you seeing yourself doing something that you are good at and seem to perform effortlessly.

## Basis #2 - Vision of some <u>Passionate Interest</u> You Desire to Pursue

This may be you seeing yourself operating in some capacity in one of your most passionate interests.

## Basis #3 - Vision of the <u>Discoveries and Occurrences</u> in Your Life

This third basis may be you seeing yourself functioning in what you are currently doing now but performing it at a higher level and greater distinction.

After you have adopted a vision for your life, which is the vision of you operating in your unique purpose, you must learn to articulate your unique purpose ---that is the description and characteristics of your life-work.

Learn to be comfortable with communicating your unique purpose. Create a written declaration that outlines what you believe you were born to do. Job 22:28 reads, *You shall also decide and decree a thing, and it shall be established for you; and the light [of God's favor] shall shine upon your ways* (**AMP**). --- then light comes.

Once you have given voice to your unique purpose, now you have begun the journey of discovering how you will execute it and live your signature life!

As you search the scriptures and meditate on God's Word concerning your unique purpose, you begin to gain understanding of how to make all the parts of your life fit and join together. God's Word gives understanding to the simple --- *The entrance of thy words giveth light; it giveth understanding unto the simple.* (**Psalms 119:130, KJV**)

Remembering the significance of the dynamic trichotomy of wisdom, knowledge and understanding will keep you on course to living the signature life that you were born to live!

**Proverbs 24:3-4** – *By wisdom a house is built, and through understanding it is established; through knowledge its rooms are filled with rare and beautiful treasures.* (**NIV**)

By *wisdom* the house is *built*... through *understanding* it is *established*...... through *knowledge* it is *filled*..

**Knowledge (parts)** → **Understanding (organize)**

→ **Wisdom (favorable results)**

**Parts** ------- **Assembly** --------- **Results**

# CHAPTER 10

∞

## Signature Thinking for Signature Living

*Finally, brethren, whatsoever things are true, whatsoever things are honest, whatsoever things are just, whatsoever things are pure, whatsoever things are lovely, whatsoever things are of good report; if there be any virtue, and if there be any praise, think on these things.   -Philippians 4:8 KJV*

As you began to actualize your signature life and fulfill your unique purpose, you are going to have to master and maintenance your thought life to thrive in signature living.

As I pointed out earlier in the book you are a unique original, there is no one exactly identical to you on earth, neither has there ever been. God has a specific work for you to do, a specific market or audience for you to serve and specific things

195

for you to create ---be it songs, books, plays, movies, technological devices, mechanical devices, cooking recipes, cures, solutions or what have you. It is your responsibility to de-clutter your thought-life and filter out all negative, counter-productive thoughts and reasoning's that would impede your progress.

Everything in your life begins as a thought and depending on the amount of time and regularity given to the thought, will determine where the thought takes you. For as a man thinks in his heart, so is he (Proverbs 23:7) ---you will become what you dwell on the most and you will end up where your thoughts consistently reside. We are all led in the direction of our most dominate thoughts. This is why we must keep diligent watch over the things we think and more specifically entertain, dwell on and give voice too.

The succession of events that occur from thought to action in a person's life usually progress as follows: ---our thoughts have a tremendous impact on our perceptions, our perceptions incite certain behaviors, these behaviors if performed consistently form habits, the habits we form overtime produce outcomes. If you desire to see different results and outcomes in your life you are going to have to begin to change the way you are thinking and what you constantly dwell on. You cannot plan to see any difference in your life if you do not do and act differently in your life ---this is first achieved in your thought-life. Your thoughts are like seeds planted, that yield a harvest of the conditions and experiences of your life.

The quickest and most effective way to change the results you are getting in your life is to change your thinking in whatever area of your life that you desire to see change. These changes are not instant but will occur overtime and will take discipline and desire to accomplish them as you experience the fruit of a renewed mind in the desired area of your life.

Your signature life requires a made up mind ---a mind that is focused with the single goal intent of fulfilling your purpose and reaching your destiny. Signature living demands a mind that has been programmed to win in life and not to accept anything less than winning. In life, winning is a decision that you must make every day. You must have the attitude that the game is not over until you win. Do not settle for less or ever sell yourself short because your worth is incomparable!

*"Signature living demands a mind that has been programmed to win in life..."*

You must know where you are headed in life and be convinced of the person whom God has made you to be and the assignment that He has purposed and tasked you with completing. Do not allow yourself to be convinced otherwise by negative, counter-productive thoughts.

On the following pages I have taken some common negative thoughts that tend to interfere with people meeting their goals and ultimately reaching their destiny. I have also listed some truths that dispel those counter-productive, negative thoughts.

## LIMITING THOUGHTS TO AVOID

**A THOUGHT:** <u>**"I'M AFRAID SO I WILL NOT TRY"**</u>

**THE TRUTH:**

- Fear is designed to contain you and paralyze you in your pursuit of destiny;

- Fear is a disconnector, it serves as a block and separating agent between you and all you desire;

- Fear is a parasitic contagious spirit that seeks to go from one person to the next ---cancelling dreams, disrupting and destroying destinies;

- Fear is a stealth enemy, many times sneaking up on its intended prey without them ever knowing.

- Most of all if you meditate fear, what you actually are doing is drawing and attracting it to you and into your world.

- Lastly, fear limits your ability to move ahead and grow.

199

# LIMITING THOUGHTS TO AVOID

## A THOUGH:
## "THERE IS NOT ENOUGH TO GO AROUND FOR EVERYONE"

## THE TRUTH:

- This idea and damning thought has its origin and root in lack and scarcity and is by extension connected to fear;

- There is always more than enough to go around and will be until the end of man's existence on earth as we know it;

- The earth was designed to reproduce and continually generate resources as long as the perpetual cycle of day and night, summer and winter and seedtime and harvest continues;

- The idea that any natural resource will ever run out is simply a deception designed to debilitate the dreamer from dreaming and to create a hoarding mentality;

200

- There is more than enough for everyone on this earth to have more than enough…that's the way God designed it to be!

## LIMITING THOUGHTS TO AVOID

## A THOUGHT:
## "I AM NOT RESPONSIBLE FOR WHAT HAPPENS TO ME"

## THE TRUTH:

- Know this, you and you only are responsible for what you do and become in your life;

- Understand that no one can stop you from reaching your destiny but YOU;

- At some point you are going to have to take full responsibility for your life;

- Blaming is to say that your right to succeed in life has been stripped from you and now you are at the mercy of the one you are blaming;

- If you are not responsible for your life and what happens to you, then who is?

- It is totally your decision to live or die, be rich or poor, succeed or fail, be healthy or sick, and increase or diminish.

## I AM

"I am" statements are positive declarations of faith concerning your place, state and stage of life. These declarations are not simply positive confessions or affirmations only but they are totally based on who God says you are and His promises for you in His Word ---the Holy Bible.

These confessions are realized in the life of the one confessing them as they speak according to their faith. According to Hebrews 11:1 in the Bible, faith is defined as the following, *Now faith is the assurance (the confirmation, the title deed) of the things [we] hope for, being the proof of things [we] do not see and the conviction of their reality [faith perceiving as real fact what is not revealed to the senses].* (**AMP**)

It is imperative that you declare with your mouth what you desire for your life out loud and not merely a silent thought alone. Mark 11:23-24 states, *Truly I tell you, whoever says to this mountain, Be lifted up and thrown into the sea! and does not doubt at all in his heart but believes that what he says will take place, it will be done for him. For this reason I am telling*

*you, whatever you ask for in prayer, believe (trust and be
confident) that it is granted to you, and you will [get it].* (**AMP**)

Notice this scripture says that it is granted to you, meaning that
upon requesting, it is released to you, however, you must
receive it by faith at that point and it shall manifest in your life.
So confessing "I am" as opposed to *I will,* confirms your
positive receipt of the declaration you have decreed.

Take time to create a list of the "I am" declarations that you
desire to see happen in your life and also use these declarations
to counter each one of the negative limiting thoughts that seem
to have become so familiar to you that you actually have begun
to believe them. Your declarations will also support who you
desire to become or what goals you desire to achieve.

When you confess "I am" you cause your subconscious mind ---
the part of you that controls 88% to 90% of your behavior to
build an image of who you desire to become , you begin a cycle
of internal positive self-talk as you set out on your destiny and
amazingly you began to attract to yourself the resources needed

to manifest the I am... declaration of your life, *i.e. being debt free, starting a business, launching a ministry, traveling around the world, feeding the hungry, building orphanages, being healthy and physically fit, becoming rich, etc.*

**Listed here are examples of the "I am" countering exercise:**

| Negative limiting thoughts | Counter I am |
| --- | --- |
| I may fail, so I will not even try | I am successful |
| I do not have enough money | I am abundantly supplied |
| I'm afraid; I have never done this before | I am fearless |
| Life is too hard | I am toil free |

# EXAMPLE OF THE "I AM" IMAGE BUILDING EXERCISE

## Declare What You Desire To Do and Become

| | |
|---|---|
| I am wealthy | I am a great public speaker |
| I am strong | I am a millionaire |
| I am debt free | I am successful |
| I am beautiful | I am creative |
| I am a winner | I am a wonderful wife |
| I am an owner | I am a high performer |
| I am a finisher | I am influential |
| I am motivated | I am increasing |
| I am a leader | I am a world traveler |
| I am strength to others | I am happy |
| I am loving | I am peaceful |
| I am gentle | I am self-control |
| I am patient | I am a Billionaire |
| I am wise | I am knowledgeable |
| I am impacting | I am witty |
| I am smart | I am a best-selling author |
| I am an award winning actor / actress | |

## Declare What You Desire To Do and Become

I am an all-star athlete       I am a top-selling salesperson

I am in great physical shape

I am calm and enjoy a full nights' sleep every night

As you speak out loud these words each day they are designed to produce pictures in your mind. The pictures that you began to envision in your mind will generate thoughts ---those thoughts create thought patterns that begin to create an image inside of you that is in some capacity linked to your unique abilities which are linked to your specific unique purpose ---this leads to you living your signature life.

If you continue to speak out daily your I am's, those images will emerge as behaviors which eventually lead to opportunities opening up for you, resources being attracted to you, key people who will be a contributor in your destiny crossing paths with you and increased capacity in your ability to think, believe and grow as you walk out your unique purpose and destiny while enjoying your signature life.

I sincerely hope that you have enjoyed the knowledge shared in this book. As you continue to discover your unique purpose in life and the great destiny that God has planned for your life that is just ahead of you, use this book as a reference tool in your library and reflect on it as you increase in the knowledge of your God ordained unique purpose and actualize your signature life.

Complete the last page of this book and keep it as a reminder of your unique purpose.

## PRECISION PURPOSE:

Enjoying the Signature Life You Were Born to Live!

### My Name:

_____

### My Unique Purpose Is:

_____

_____

_____

### Date I Discovered My Purpose

_____

## About the Author

Osazee O. Thompson is a visionary leader, empowering motivator, speaker, author, success trainer, business consultant and life coach. For more than a decade, Osazee has been doing the work to see positive change in the lives of the people he serves. He has a sincere passion and desire to see people thrive in their purpose and live their dreams. Osazee addresses issues that have an impact on all humankind fulfilling their purpose and reaching their God-ordained destiny. He is the founder and President of LifeNett Works leadership & business strategy consulting company and founder and Chairman of The International School of Purpose. Osazee coaches, consults, trains and mentors people to discover and actualize their God-given purpose and to fulfill their dreams, accomplish the goals they have set for themselves and reach their highest potential. Osazee earned his Bachelor degree from Chicago State University and is also a graduate of the Joseph Business School. He received his Life Coaching certification from the Youth and Family Guidance Institute. Osazee has also produced other self-help and business publications to enhance the development and growth of all who utilize them. Osazee is a United States Marine Corps veteran. He is married and has one daughter.

For this and other books, audio programs and personal development resources you may purchase from the *Online Store* page at

www.OsazeeThompson.com

**Connect with Osazee through social media:**

www.**facebook**.com /OsazeeOThompson

www.**twitter**.com/OsazeeThompson

www.**linkedin**.com/in/OsazeeThompson

www.**youtube**.com/user/OsazeeThompson

To request Osazee O. Thompson to speak at your next conference, seminar or as the keynote speaker at your upcoming event, please contact our booking line at:

(312) DES-TINY (337-8469).

# End notes

1. www.en.wikipedia.org/wiki/energy

2. www.learner.org/interactives/renaissance/printing.html

3. www.abrahamlincolnonline.org/lincoln/speeches/quotes.htm

4. British Medical Journal source reference: Tsai et al, "Age at retirement and long term survival of an industrial population: prospective cohort study," BMJ, Published online Oct.20, 2005

5. csep10.phys.utk.edu/astr161/lect/history/newton3laws.html

6. communicationtheory.org/aristotles-communication-model/

7. www.goodreads.com/quotes/29612-character

8. www.brainyquote.com/quotes/authors/m/martin_luther.html

9. www.entreprenuer.com/article/197544

10. northbysouth.kenyon.edu/1998/edu/home/btw.htm

11. www.biography.com/people/booker-t-washington-9524663

12. en.wikipedia.org/wiki/Albert_Lutuli

13. en.wikipedia.org/wiki/Mother_Teresa

14. www.infoplease.com/ipa/A0001328.html

15. www.unitedway.org/pages/history/

16. www.redcross.org/about-us/history

17. en.wikipedia.org/wiki/self-actualization

PRECISION PURPOSE